Real World
Colouring Book
For Advanced Users & Adults

50 Images

**Created From Real Life Photos
For You To Colour As You Please.**

ISBN 978-0-359-93601-4

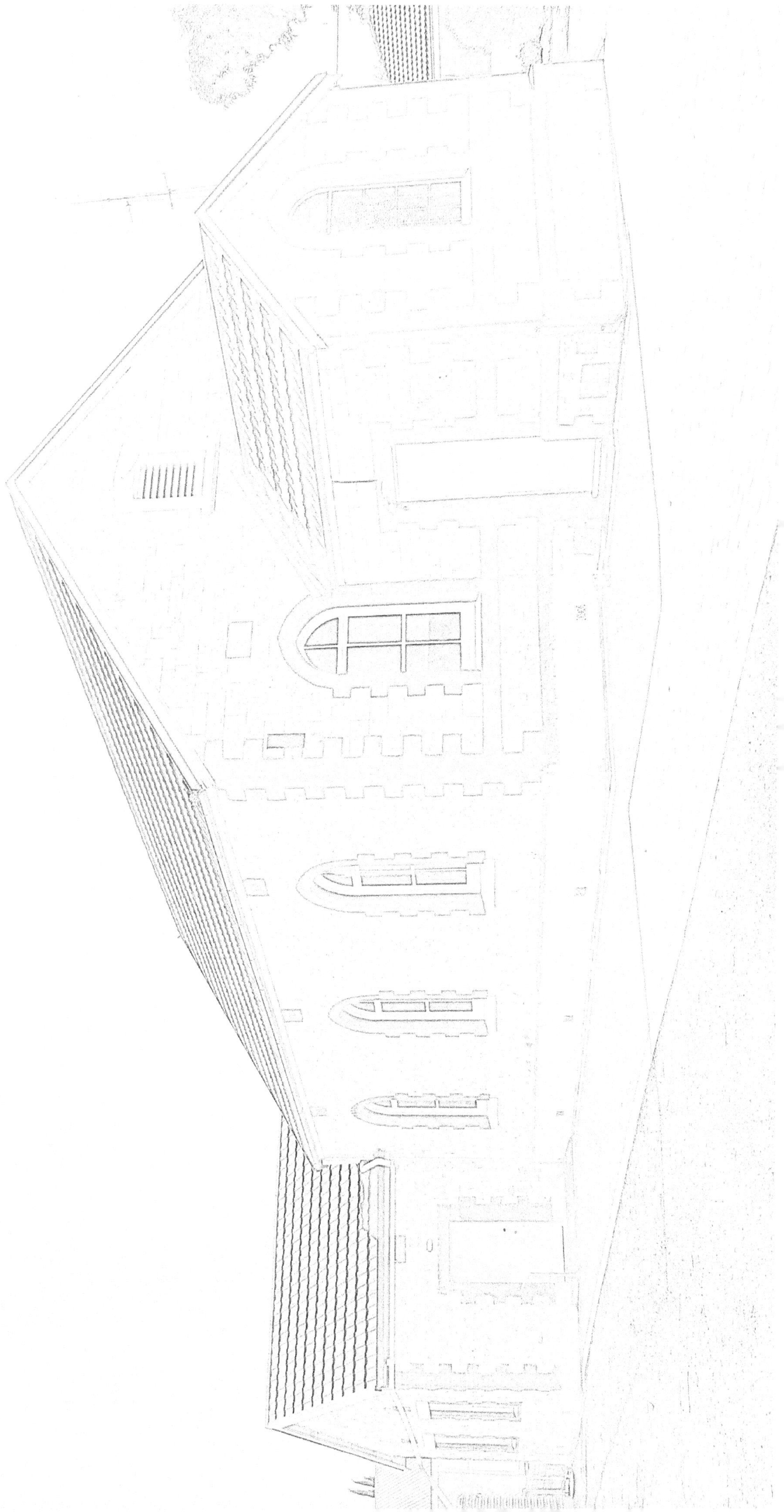

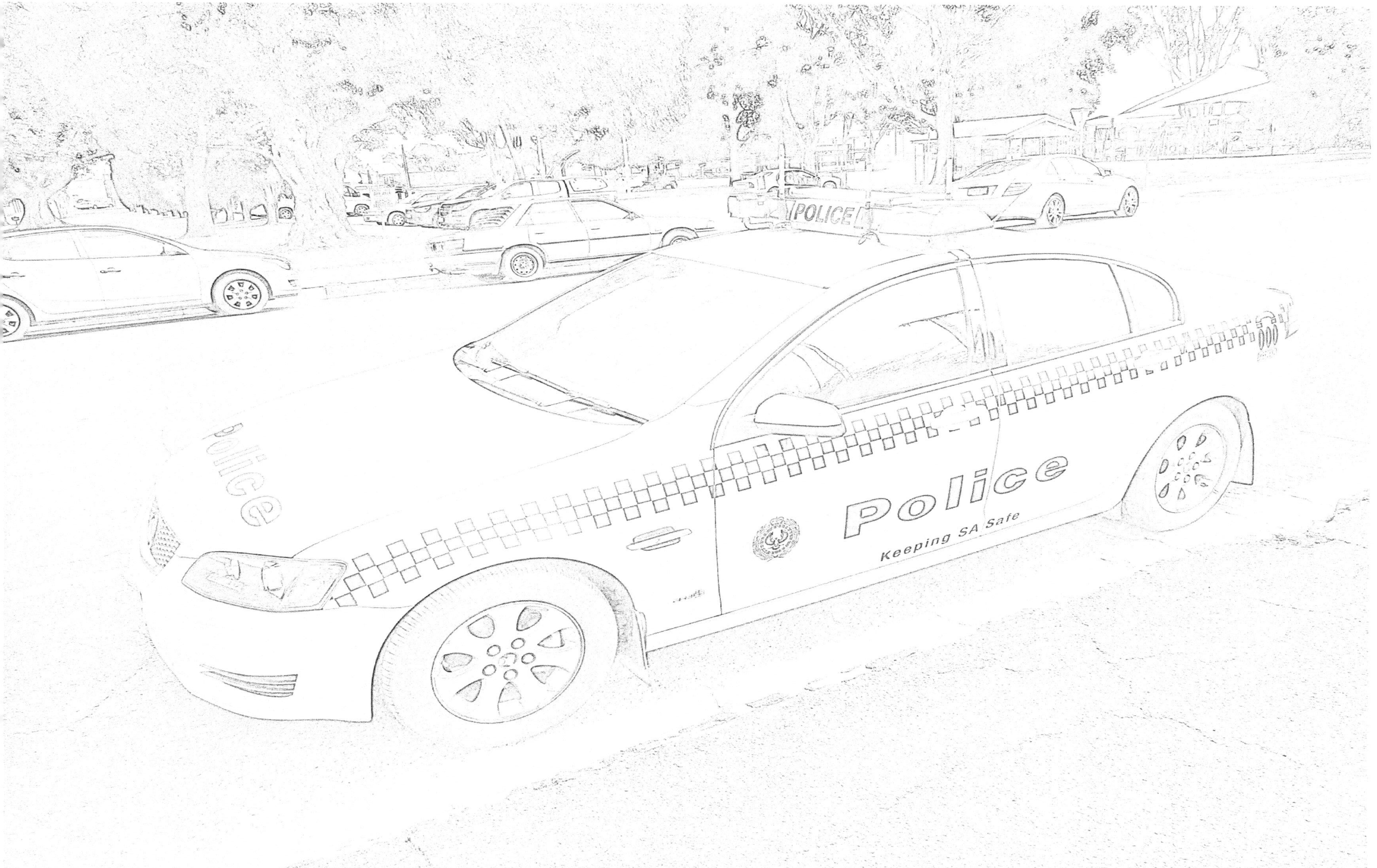
POLICE
Police
Police
Keeping SA Safe

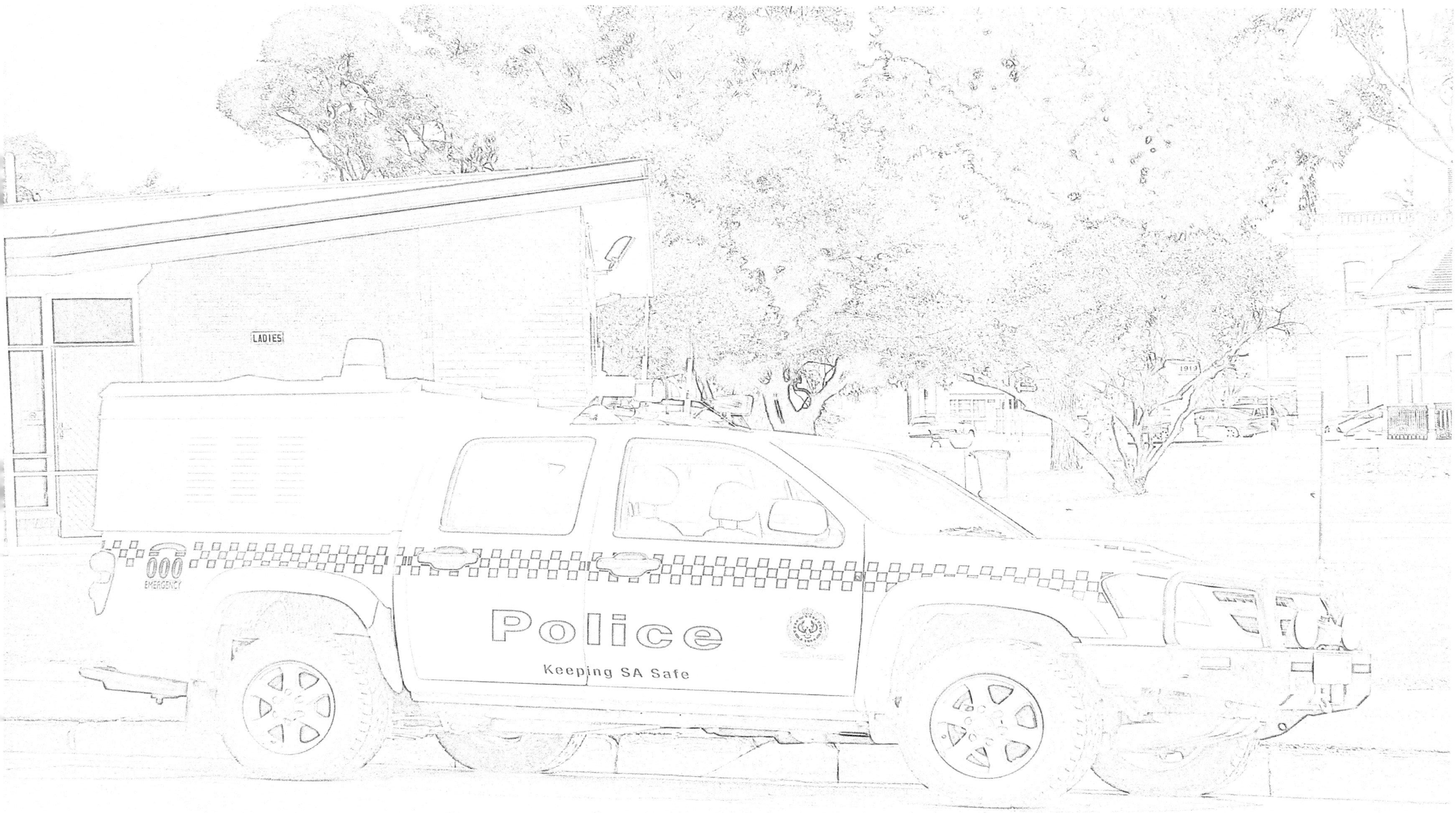
LADIES
000
EMERGENCY
Police
Keeping SA Safe
1913

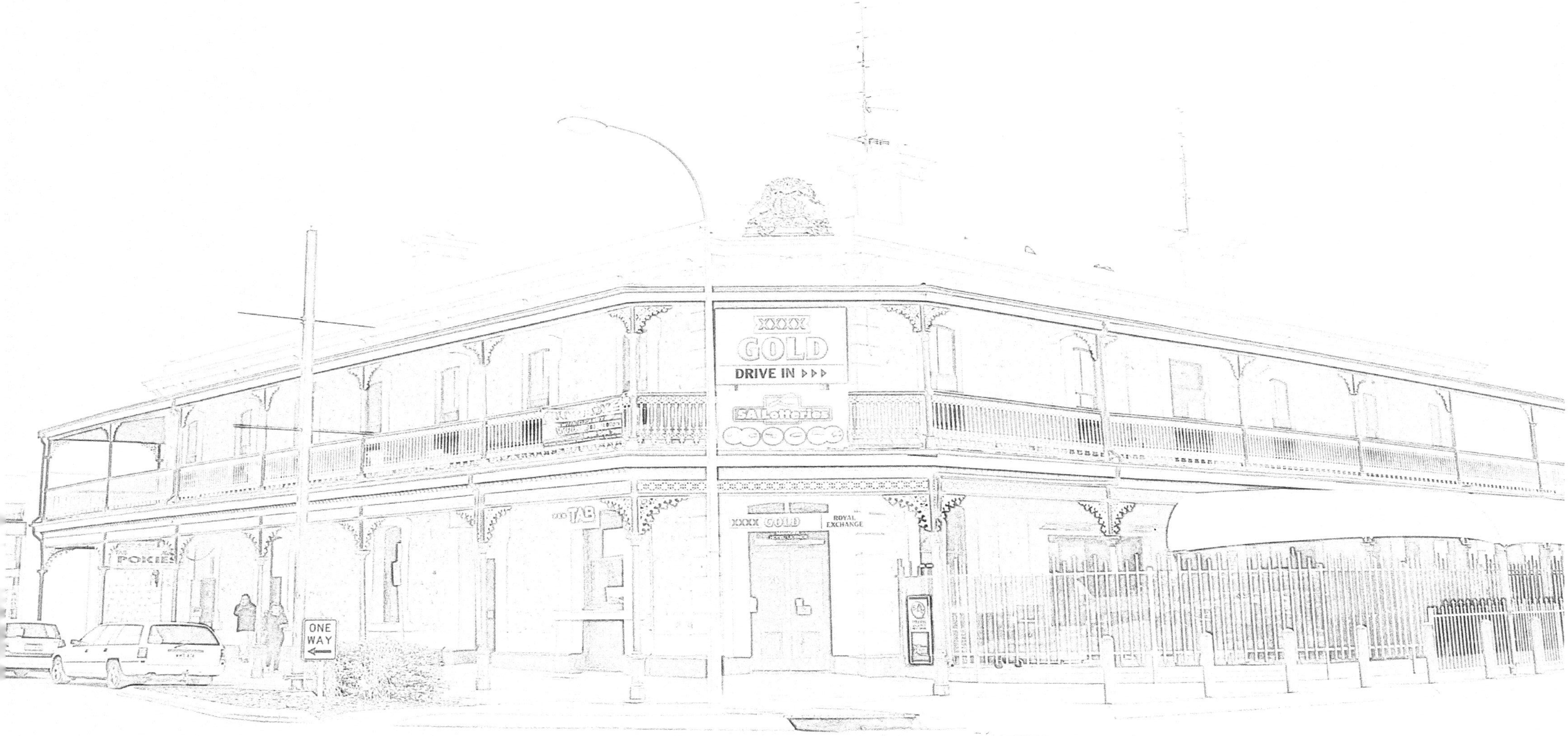
XXXX
GOLD
DRIVE IN
SA Lotteries
TAB
XXXX GOLD
ROYAL EXCHANGE
POKIES
ONE WAY

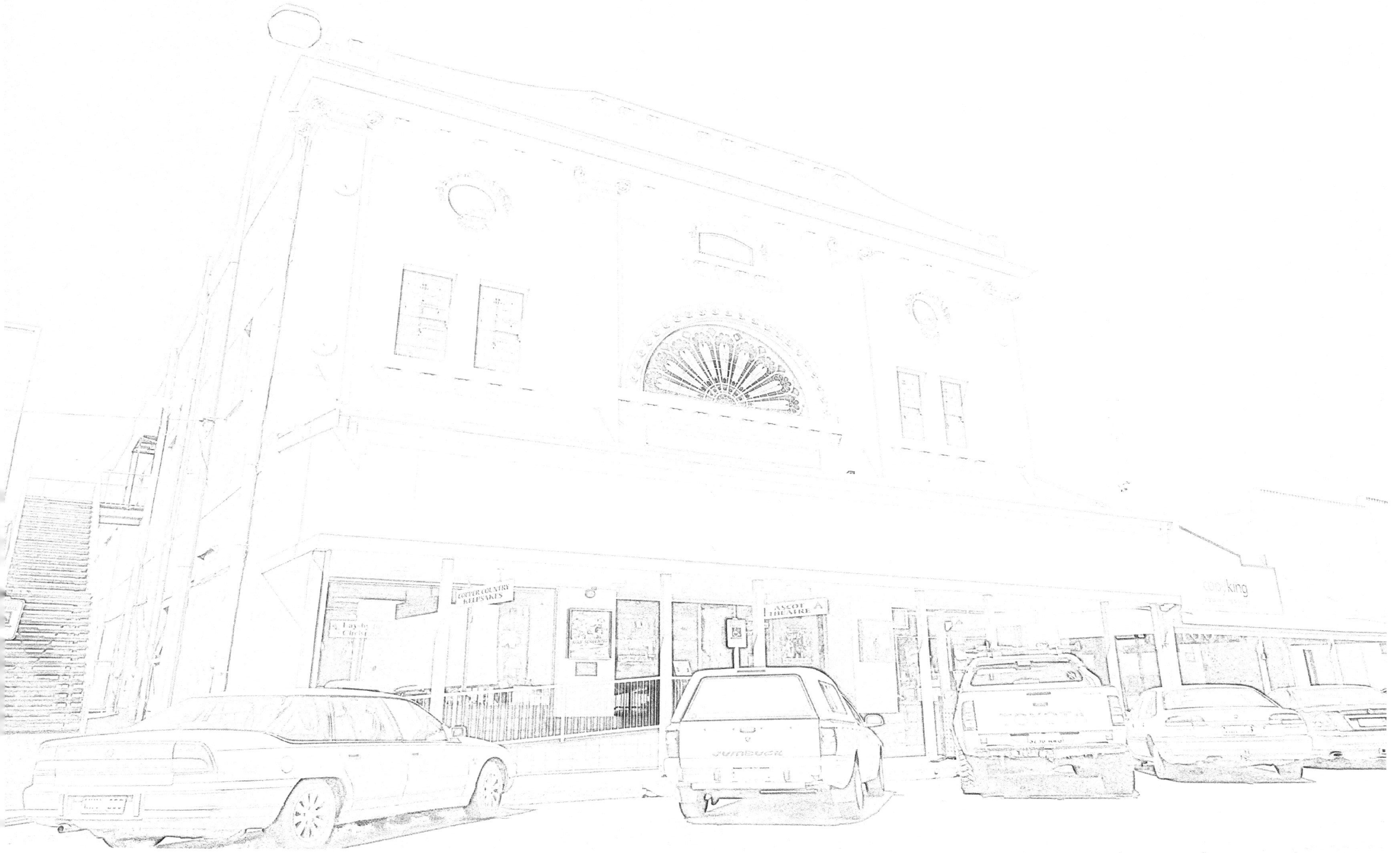
COPPER COUNTRY KEEPSAKES
ASCOT THEATRE
JUMBUCK

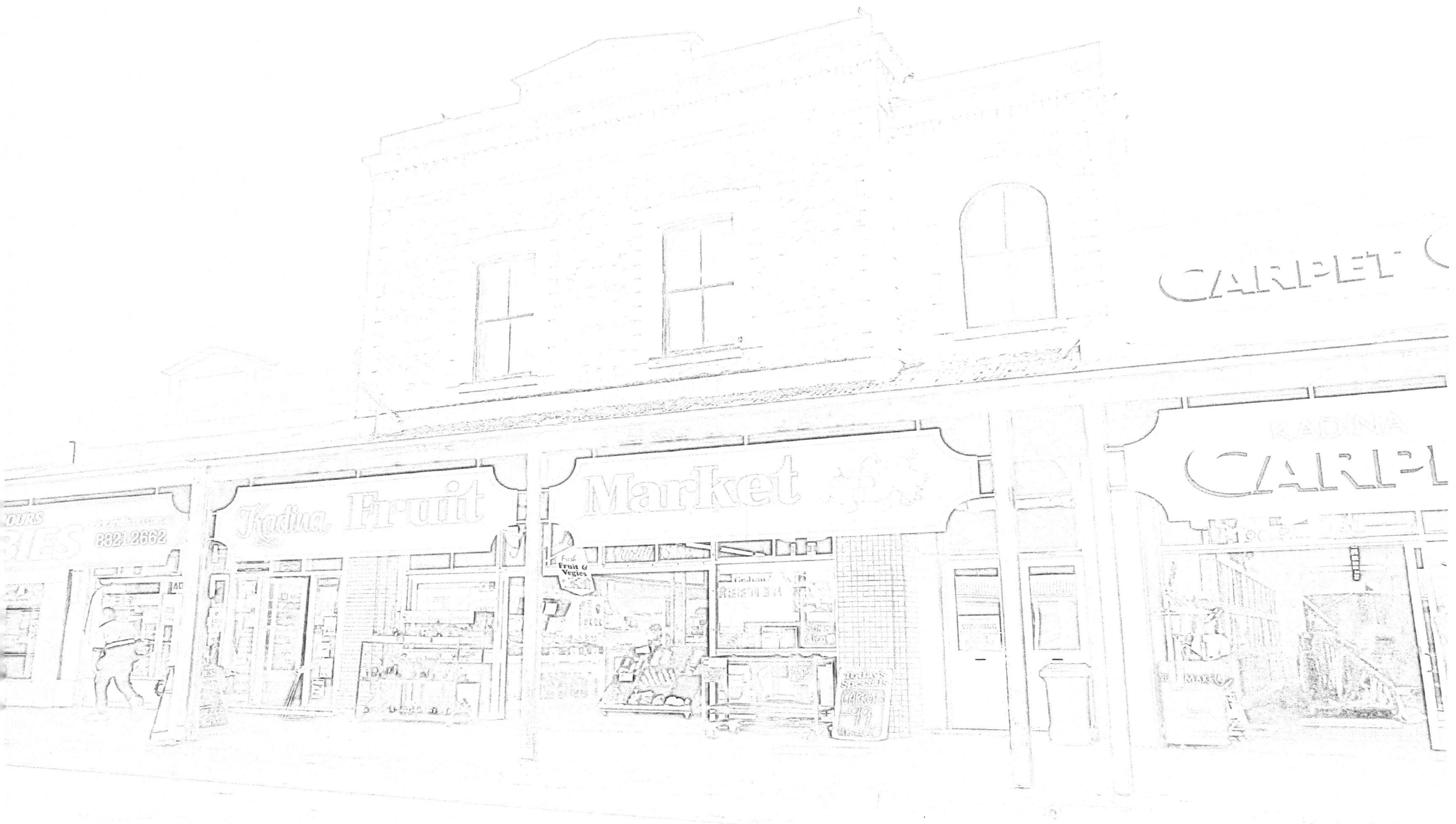
CARPET
Kadina Fruit
Market
Fresh Fruit & Vegies
8821 2662
KADINA
CARPET

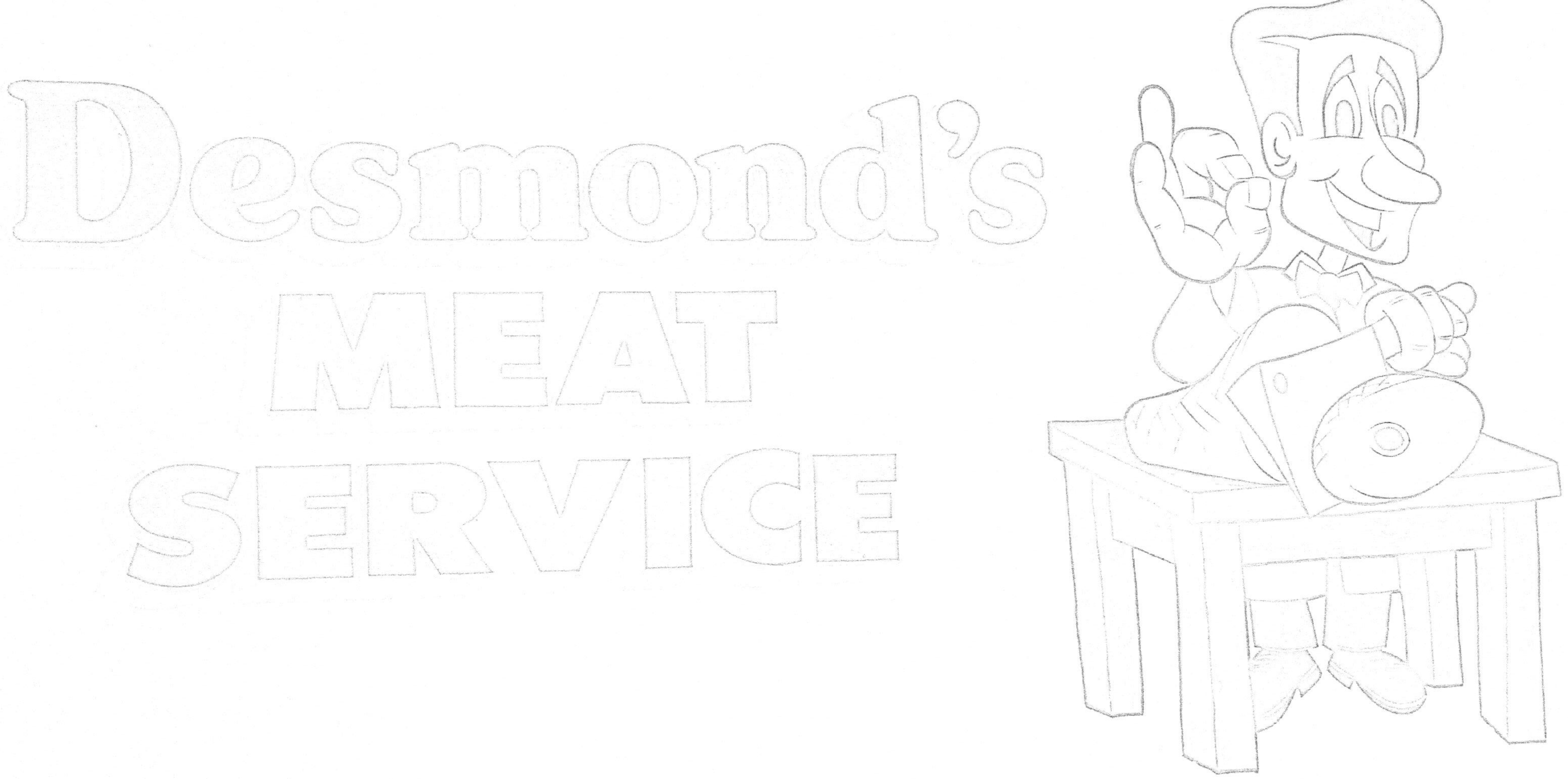
Desmond's
MEAT
SERVICE

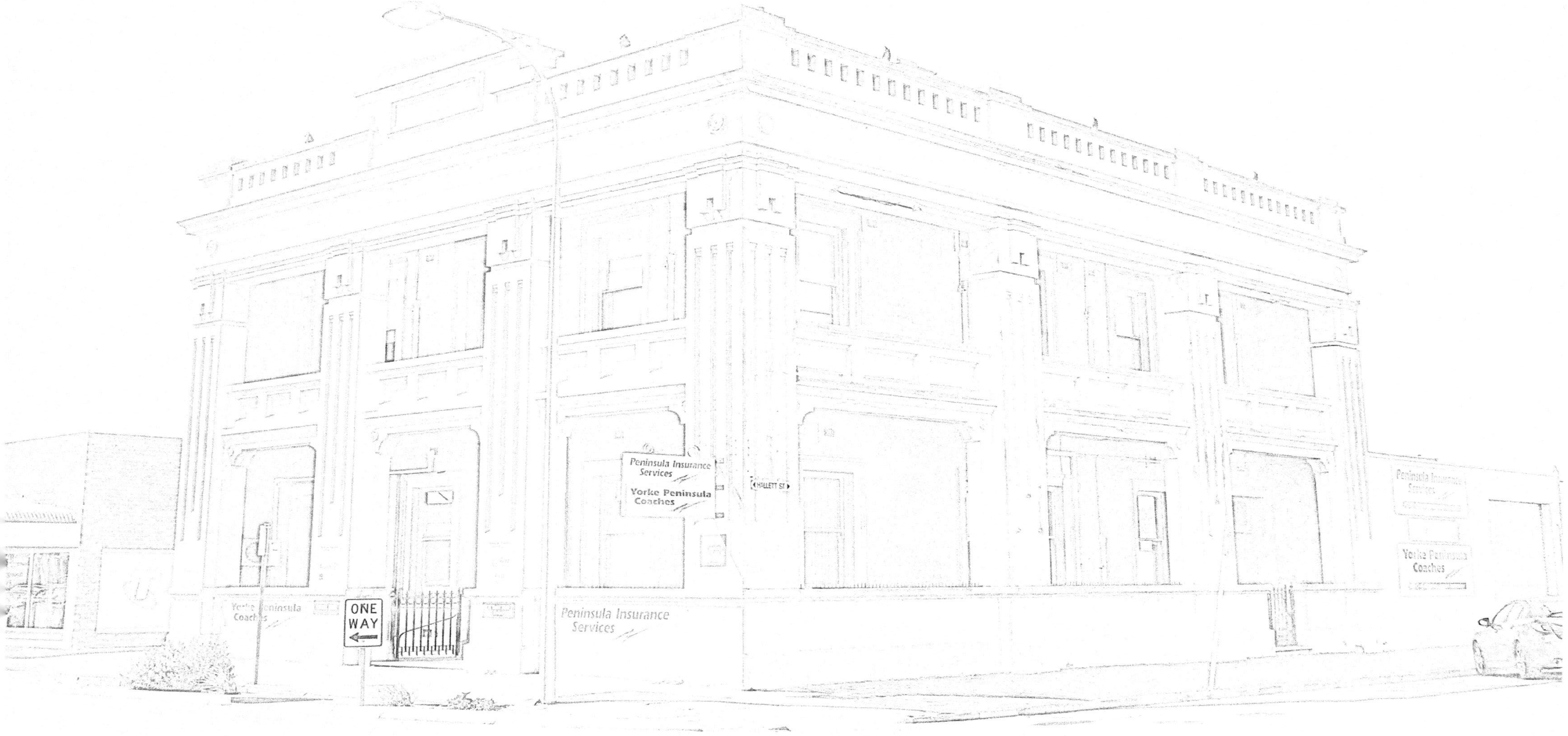

Peninsula Insurance
Services
Yorke Peninsula
Coaches
HALLETT ST
ONE
WAY
Peninsula Insurance
Services

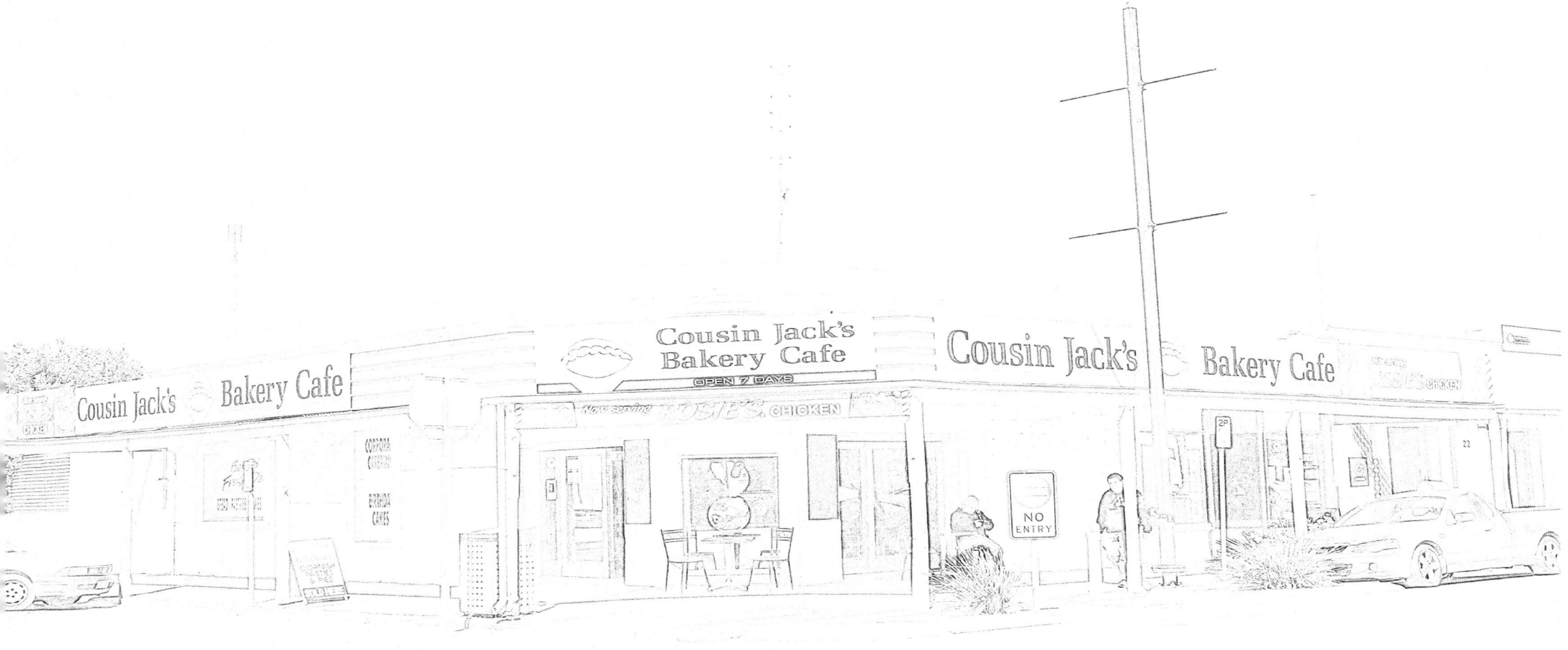
Cousin Jack's Bakery Cafe
Cousin Jack's
Bakery Cafe
OPEN 7 DAYS
Now serving ROSIE'S CHICKEN
Cousin Jack's Bakery Cafe
NO ENTRY
2P

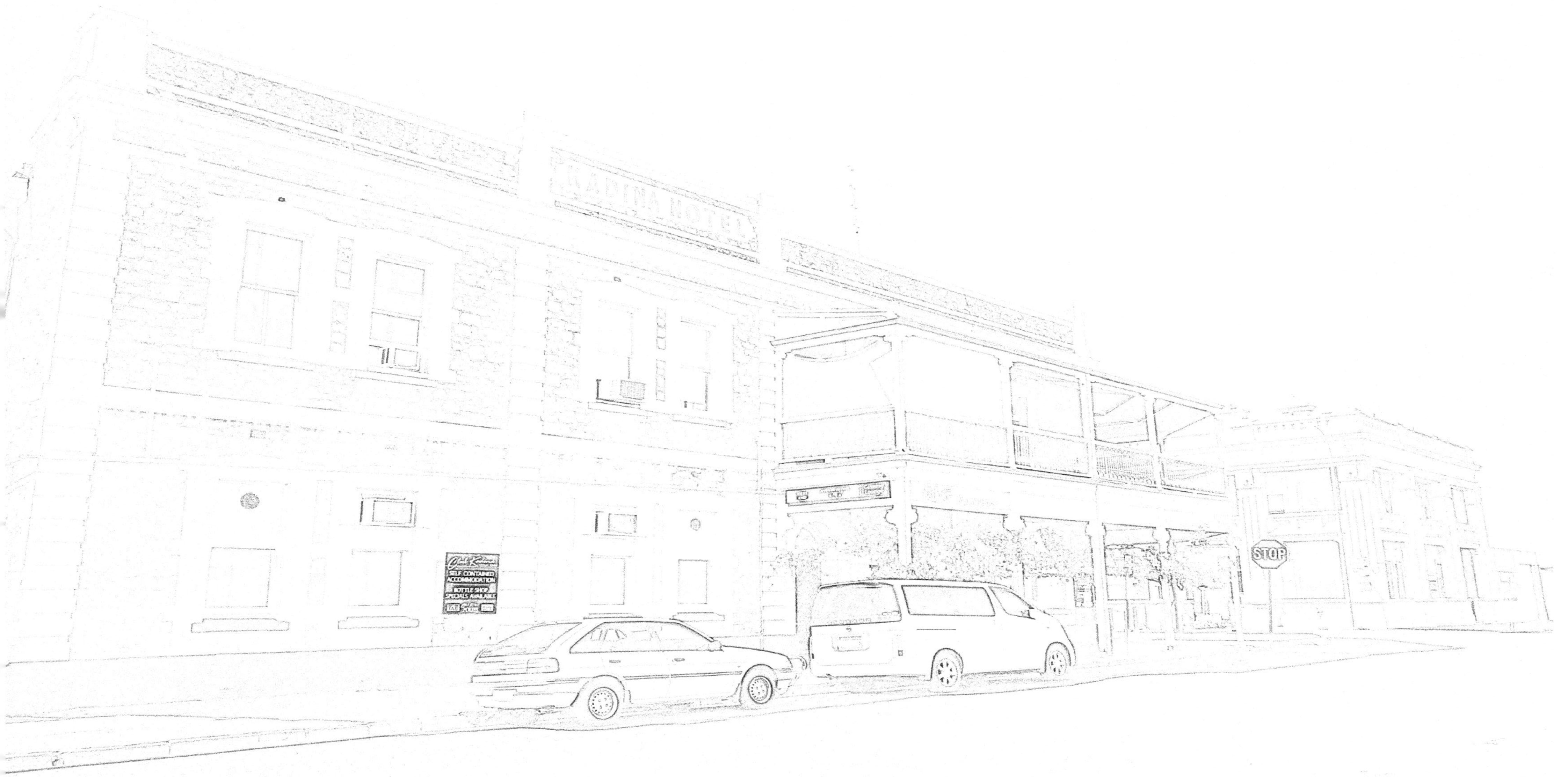
SELF CONTAINED
ACCOMMODATION
BOTTLE SHOP
SPECIALS AVAILABLE
STOP

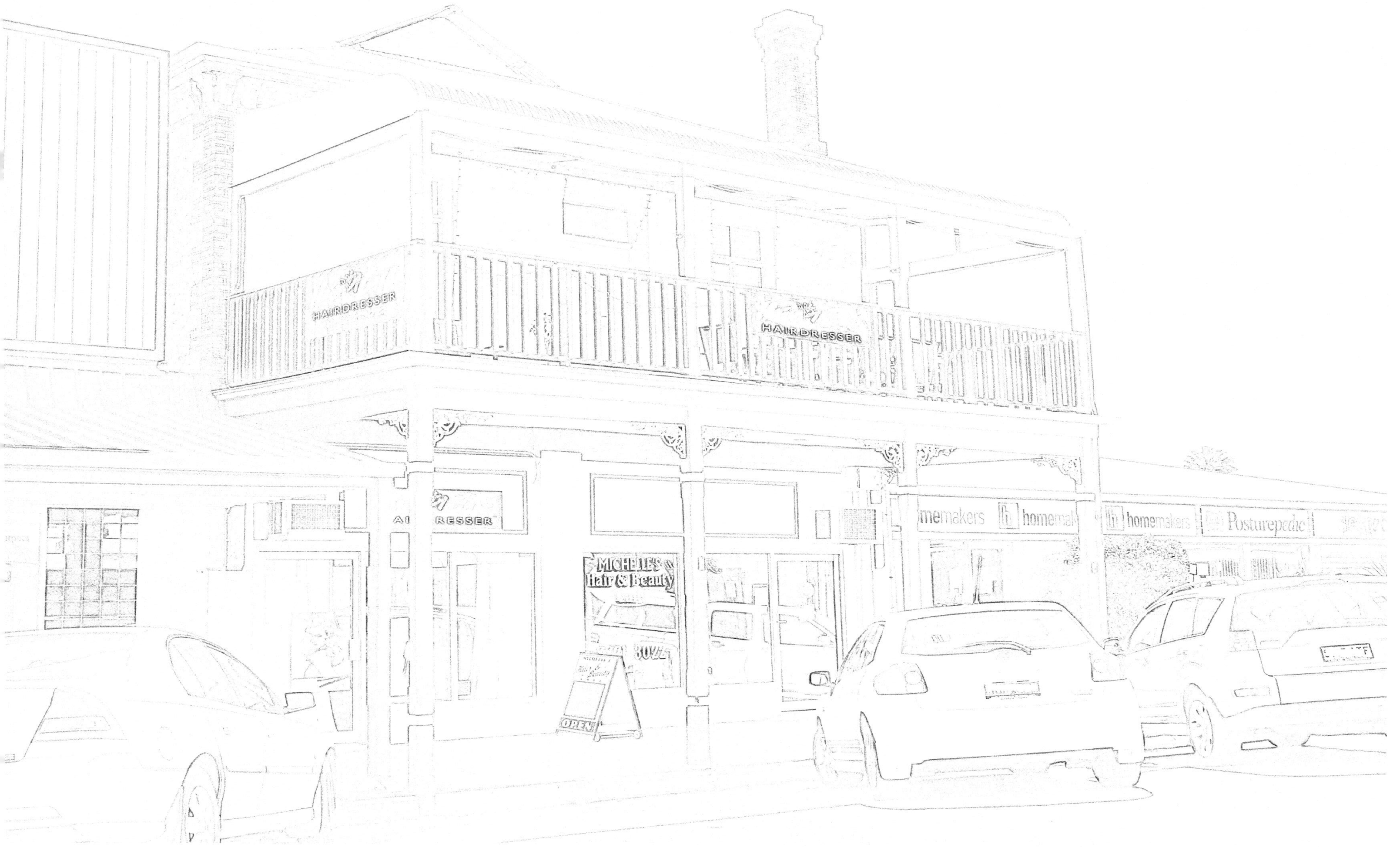
HAIRDRESSER
HAIRDRESSER
RESSER
MICHELLE'S
Hair & Beauty
OPEN
homemakers
homemakers
Posturepedic

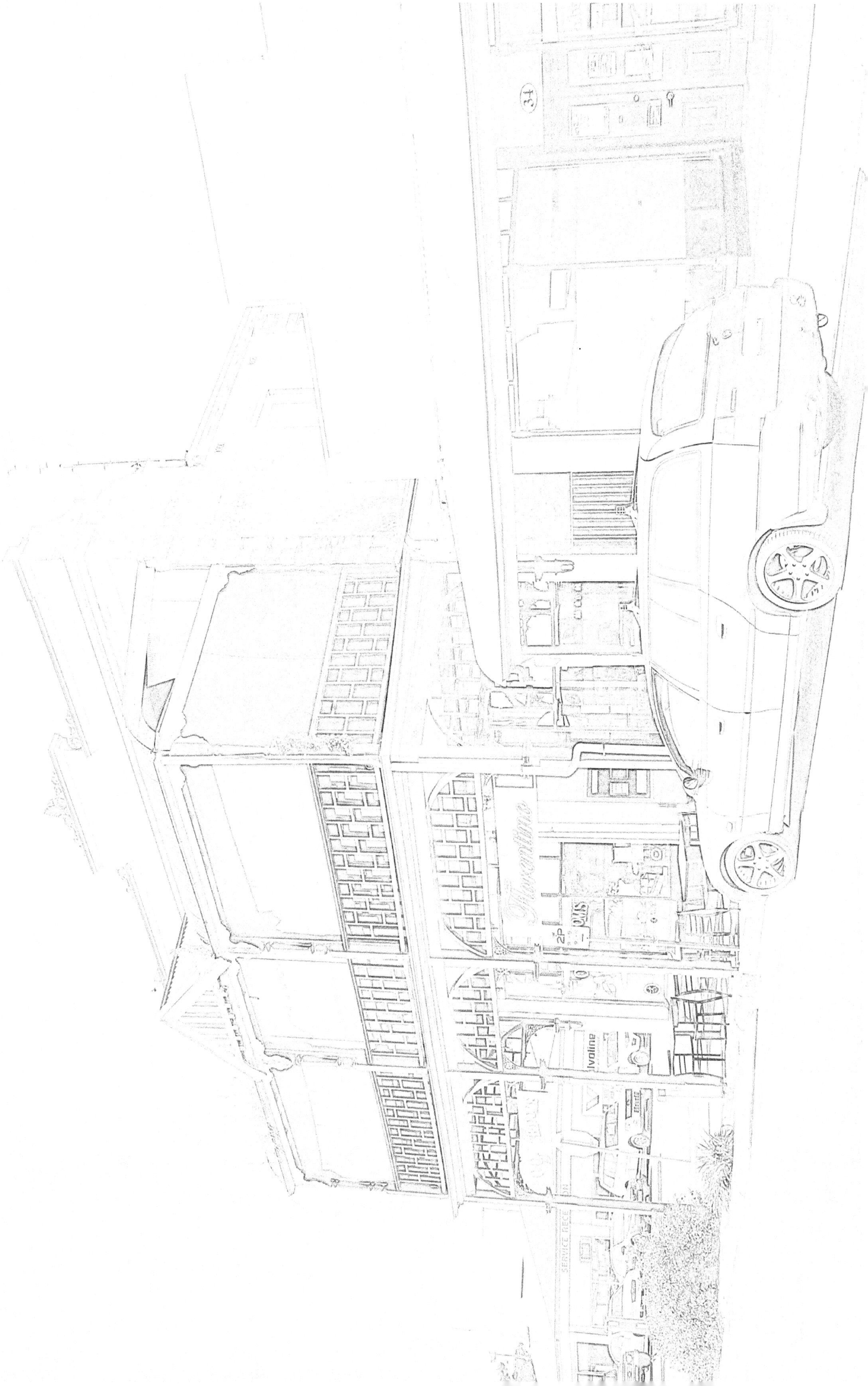

Ray White
Ray White
Ray White
Ray White
2P

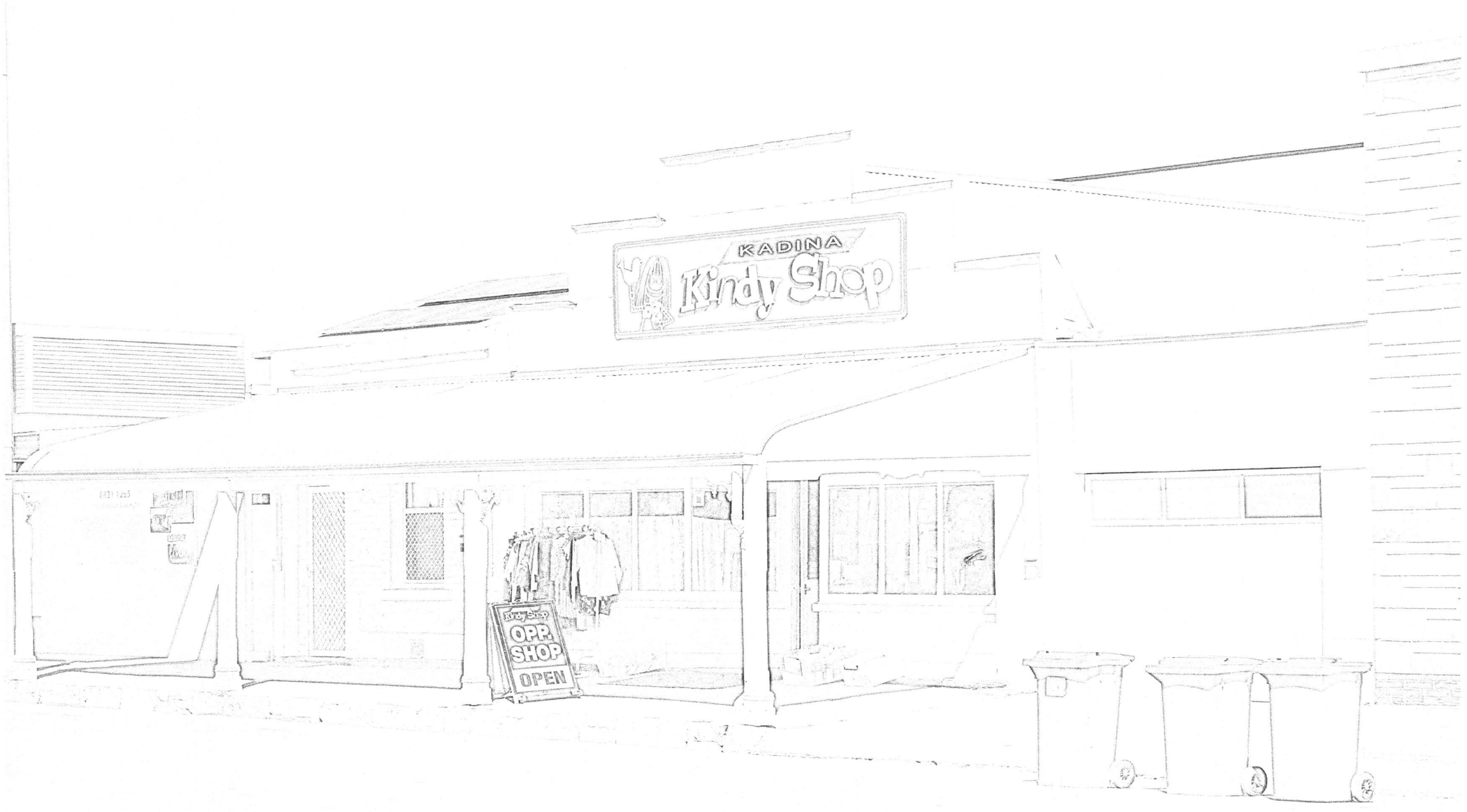
KADINA
Kindy Shop
Kindy Shop
OPP. SHOP
OPEN

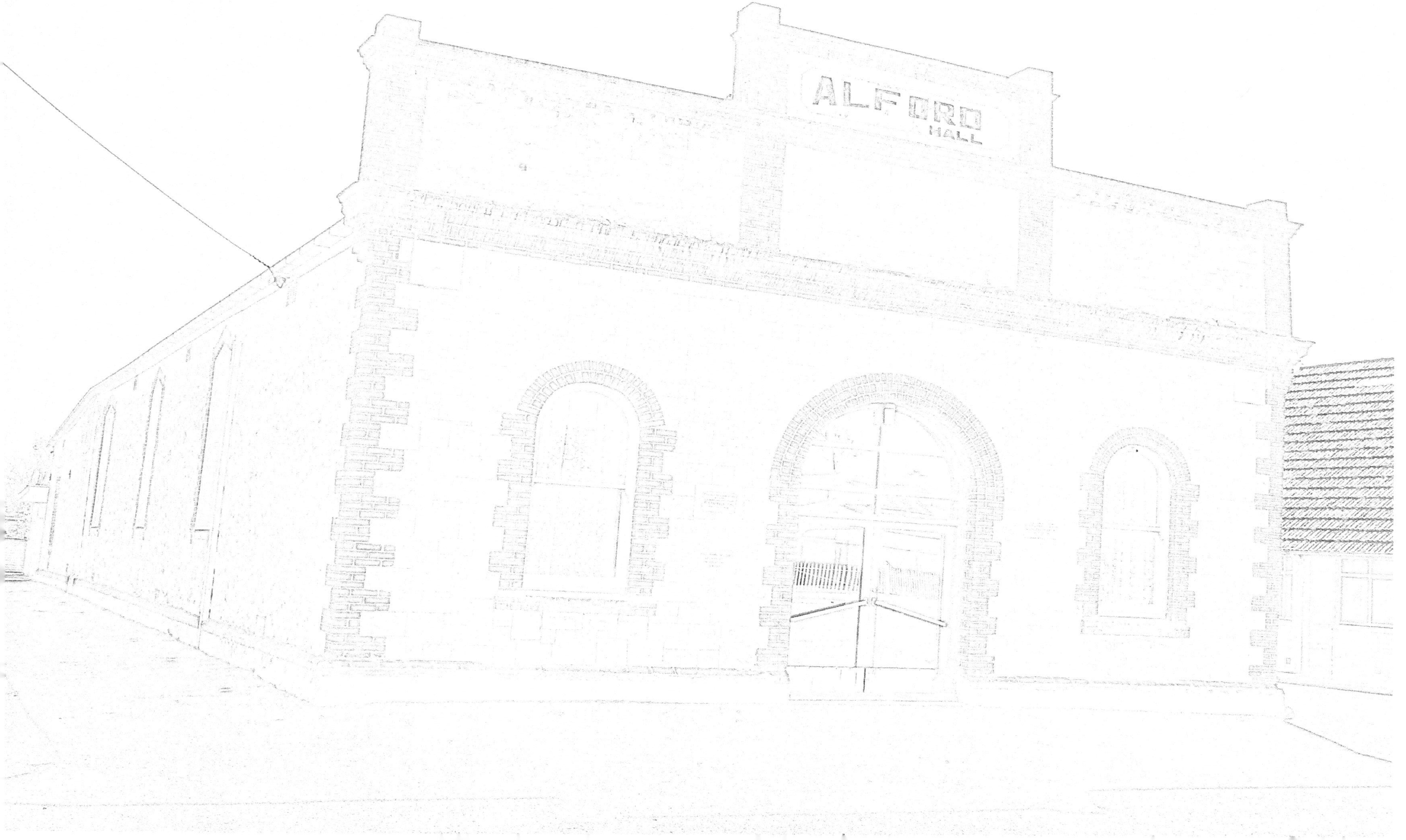
ALFORD
HALL

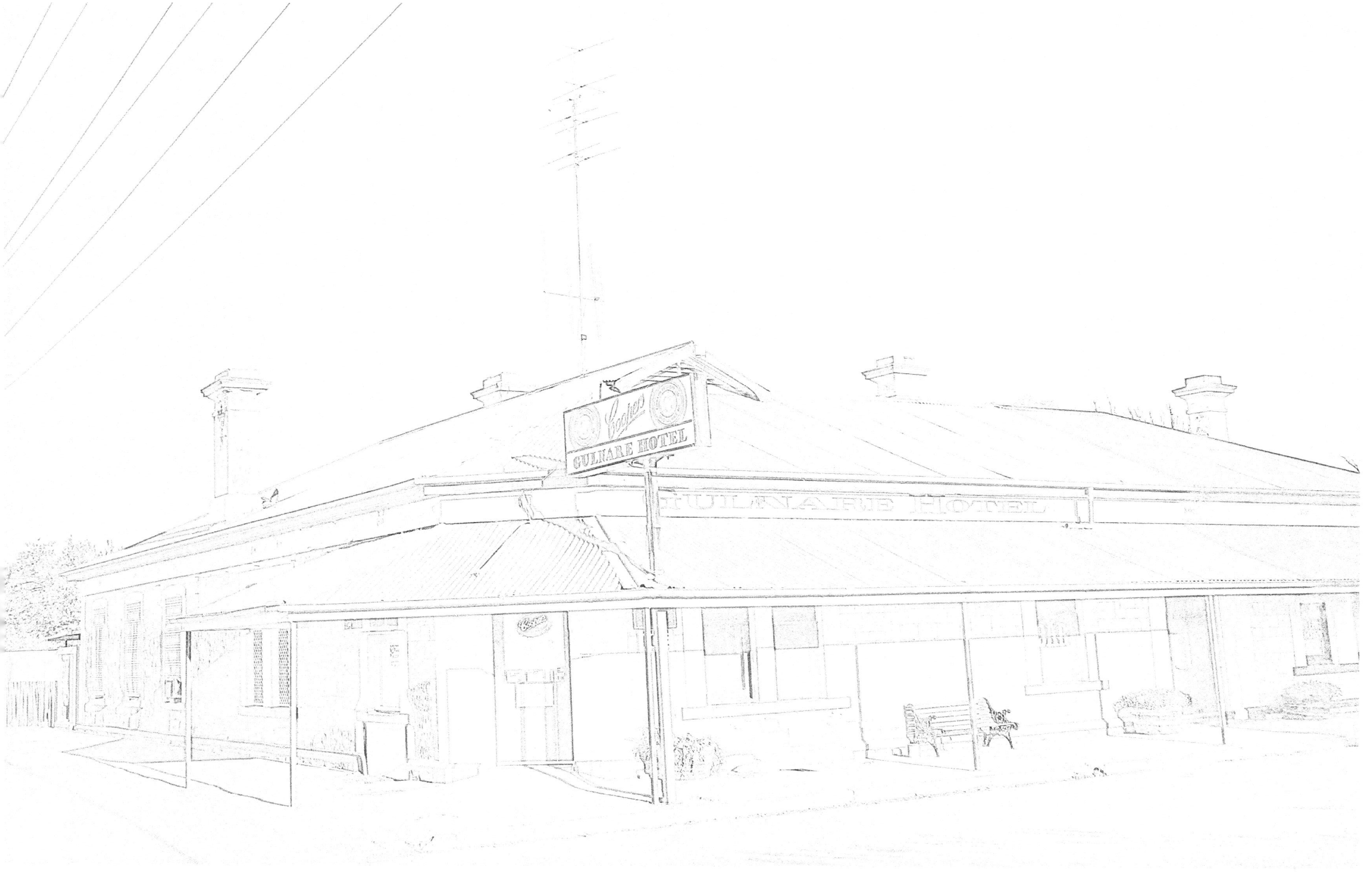
Coopers
GULNARE HOTEL

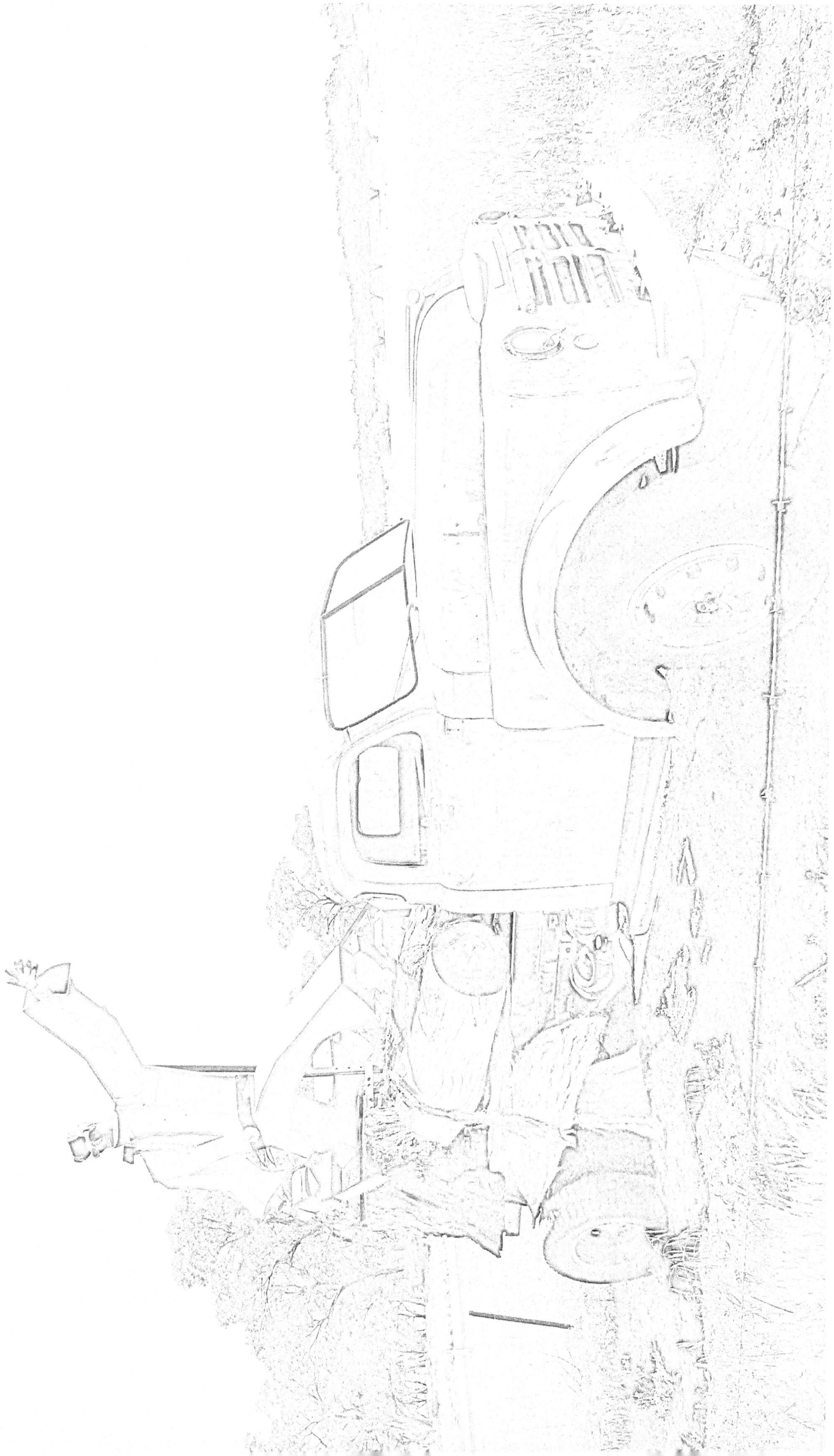

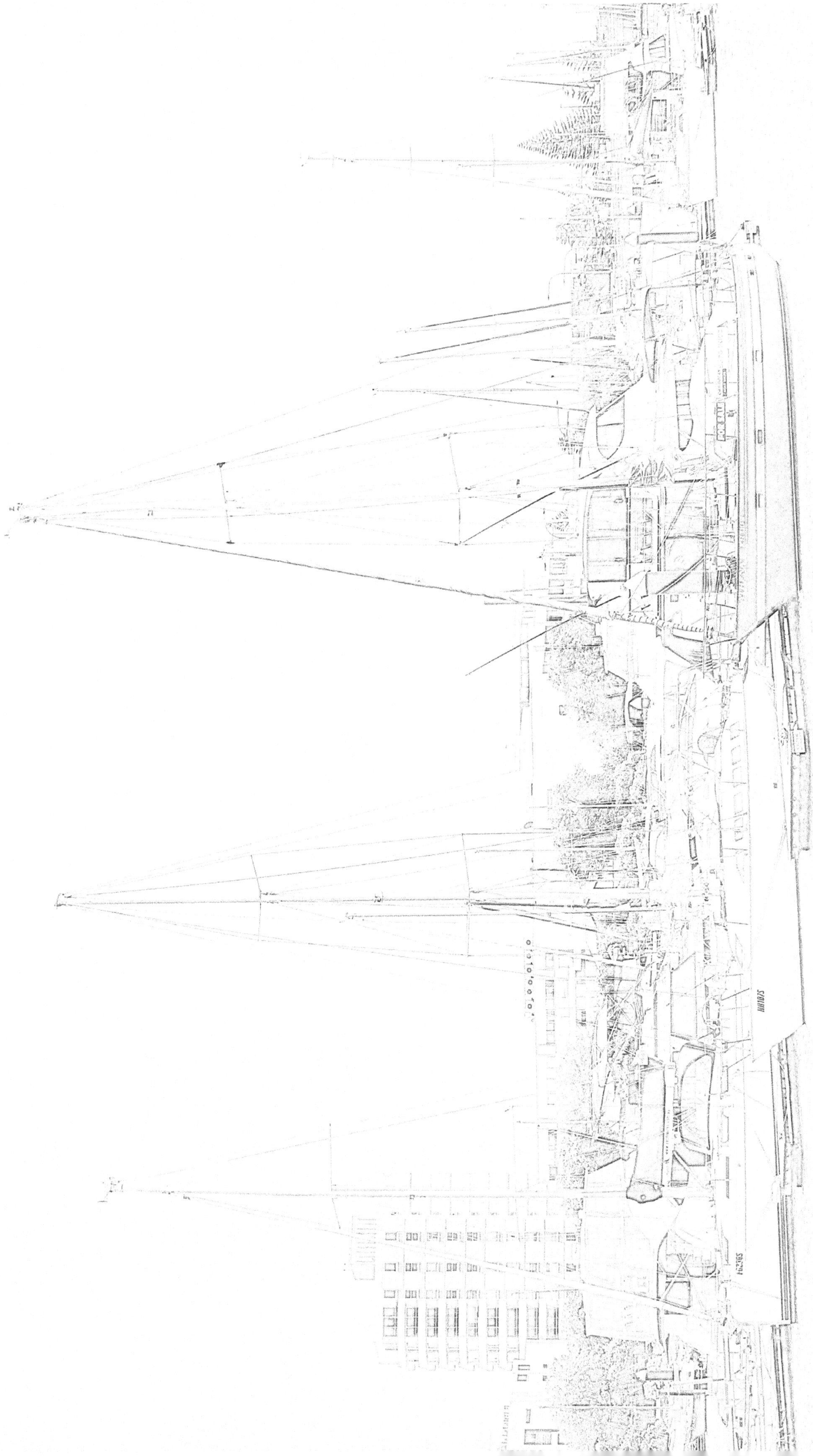

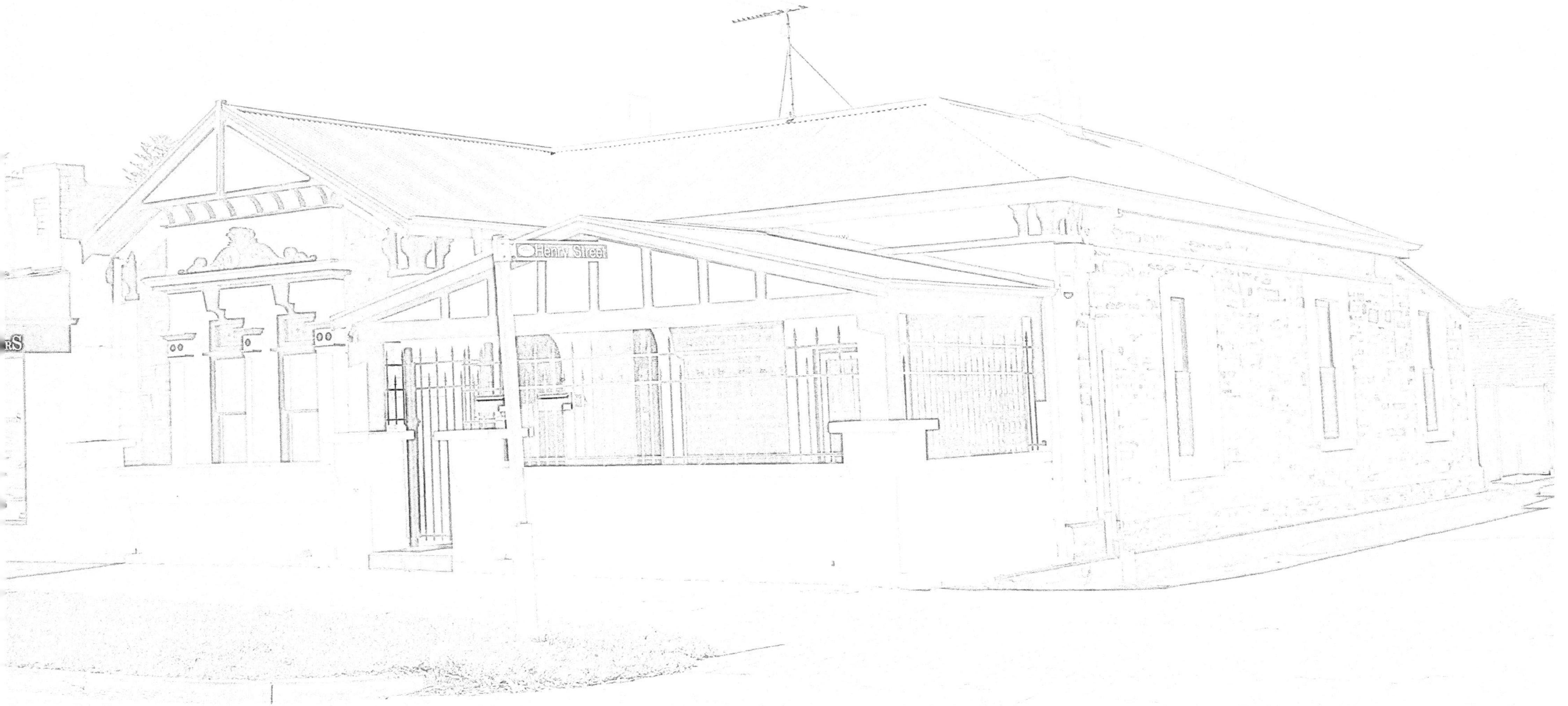
Henry Street

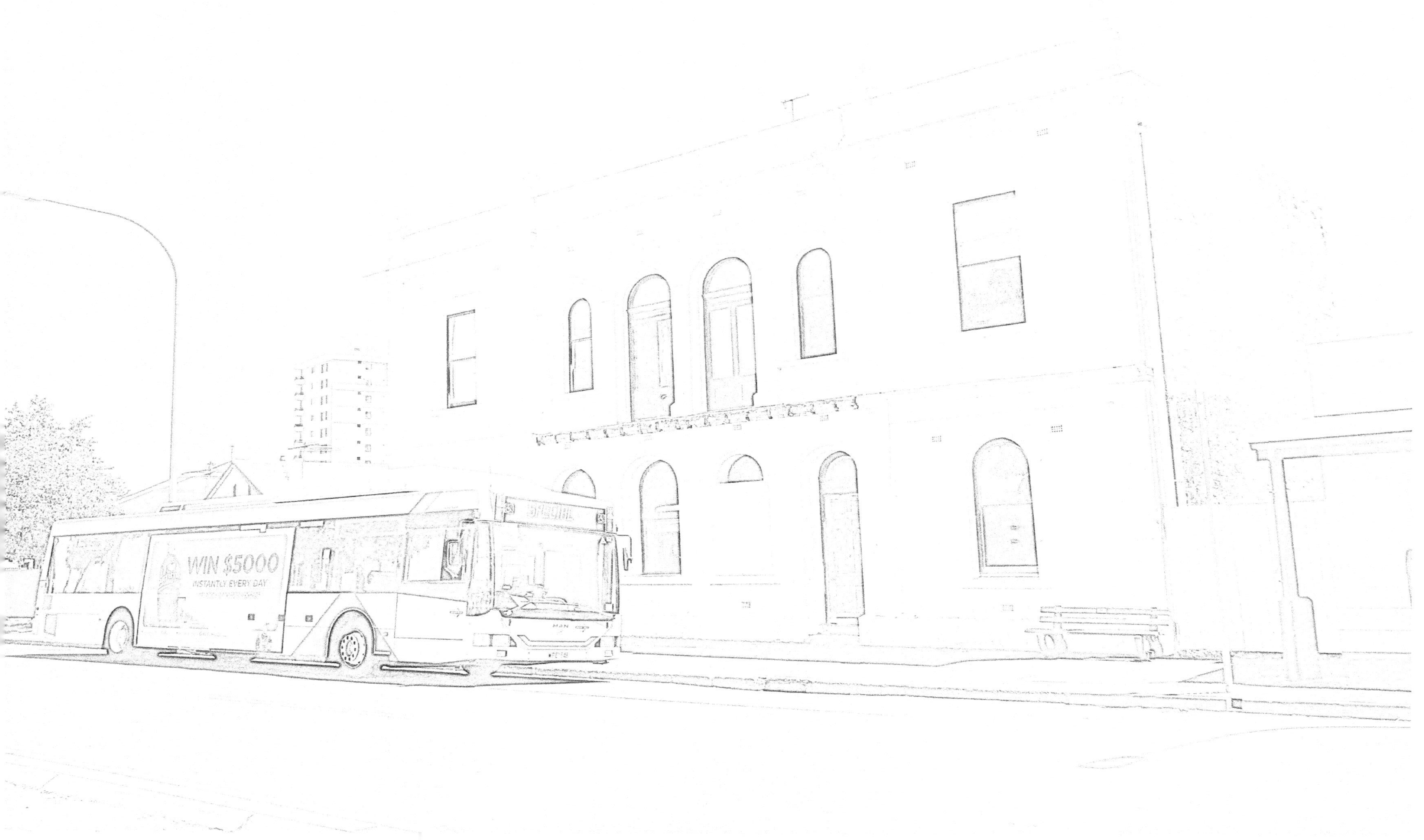
WIN $5000
INSTANTLY EVERY DAY

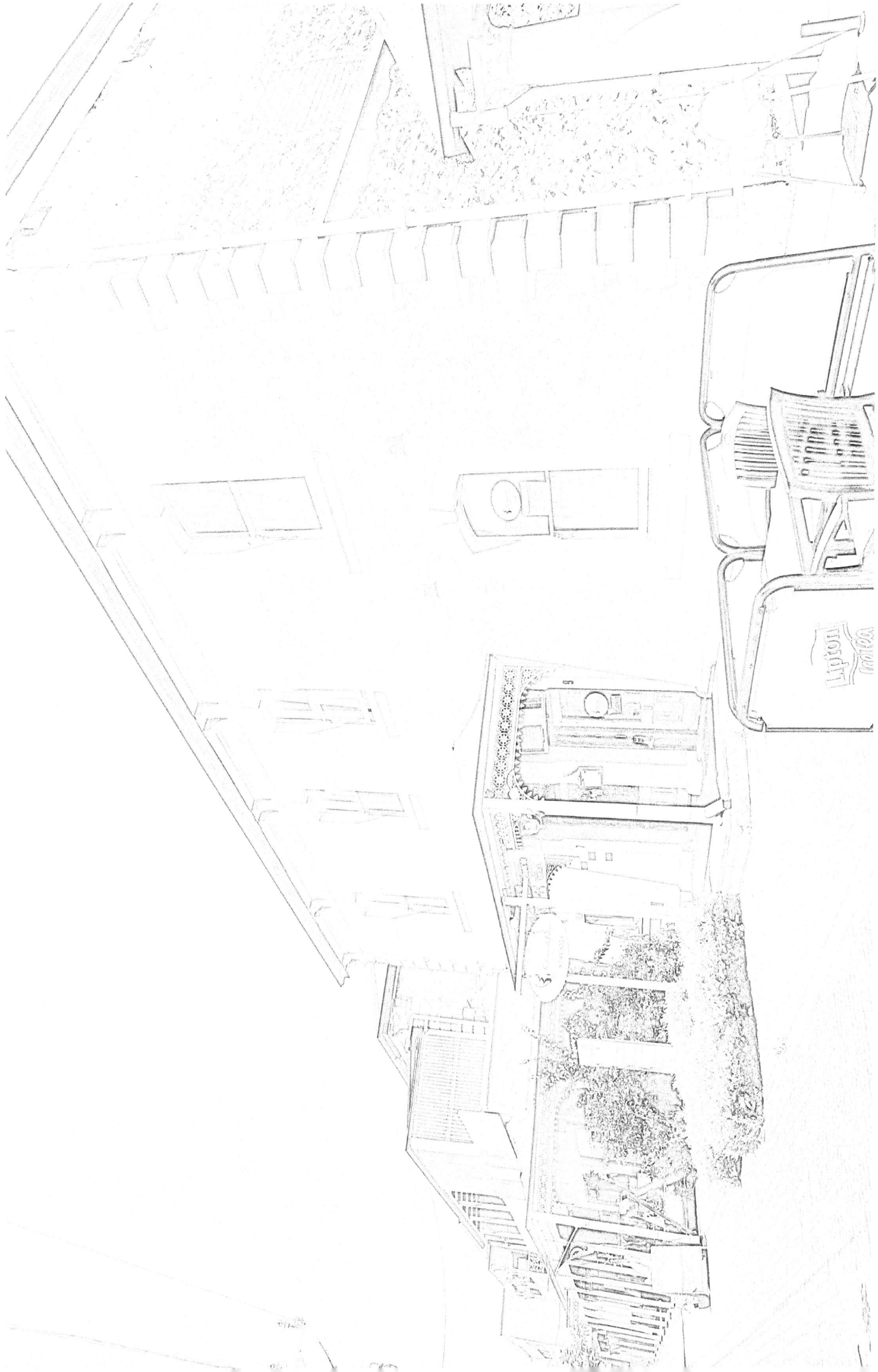
Lipton

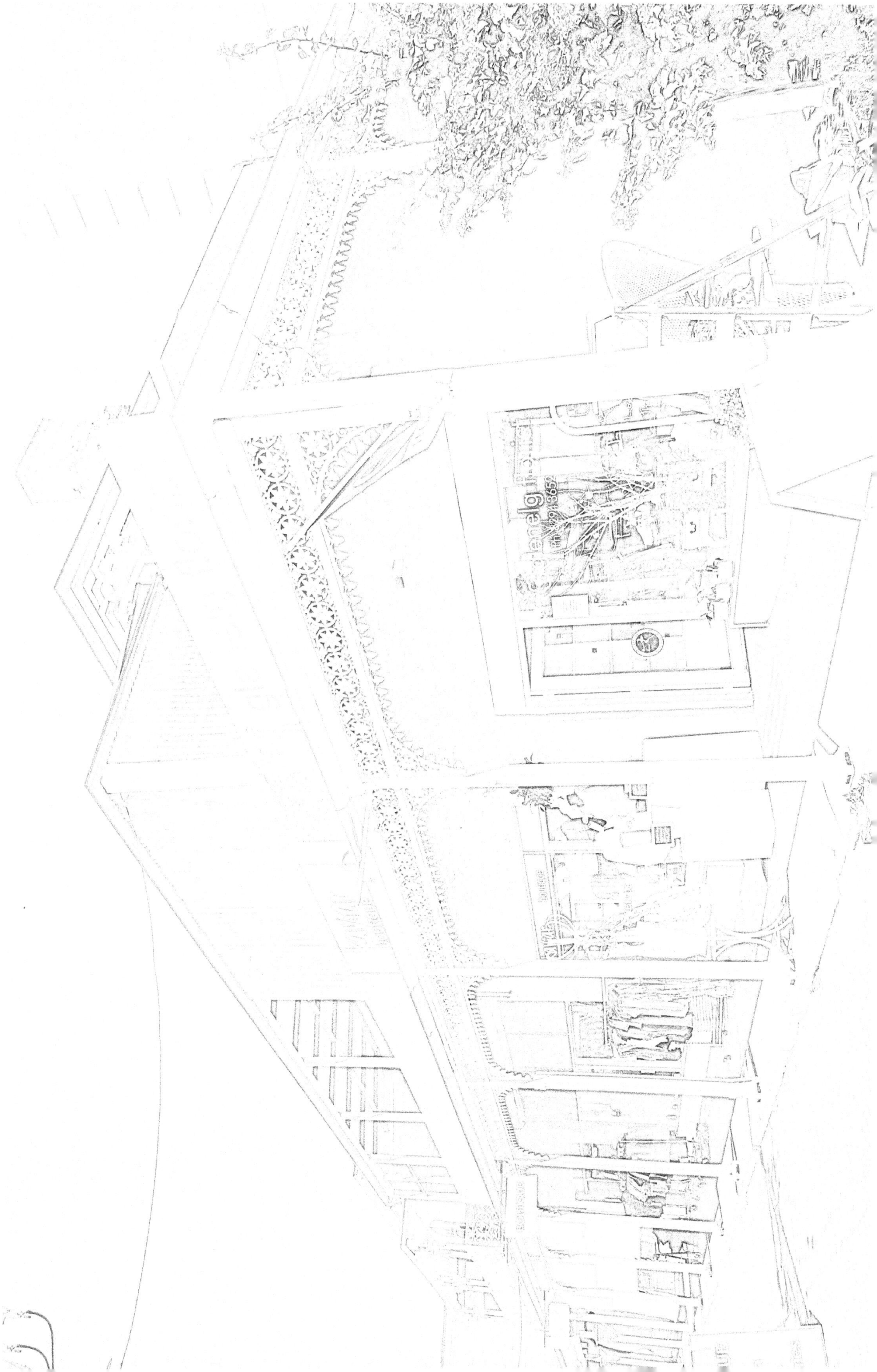

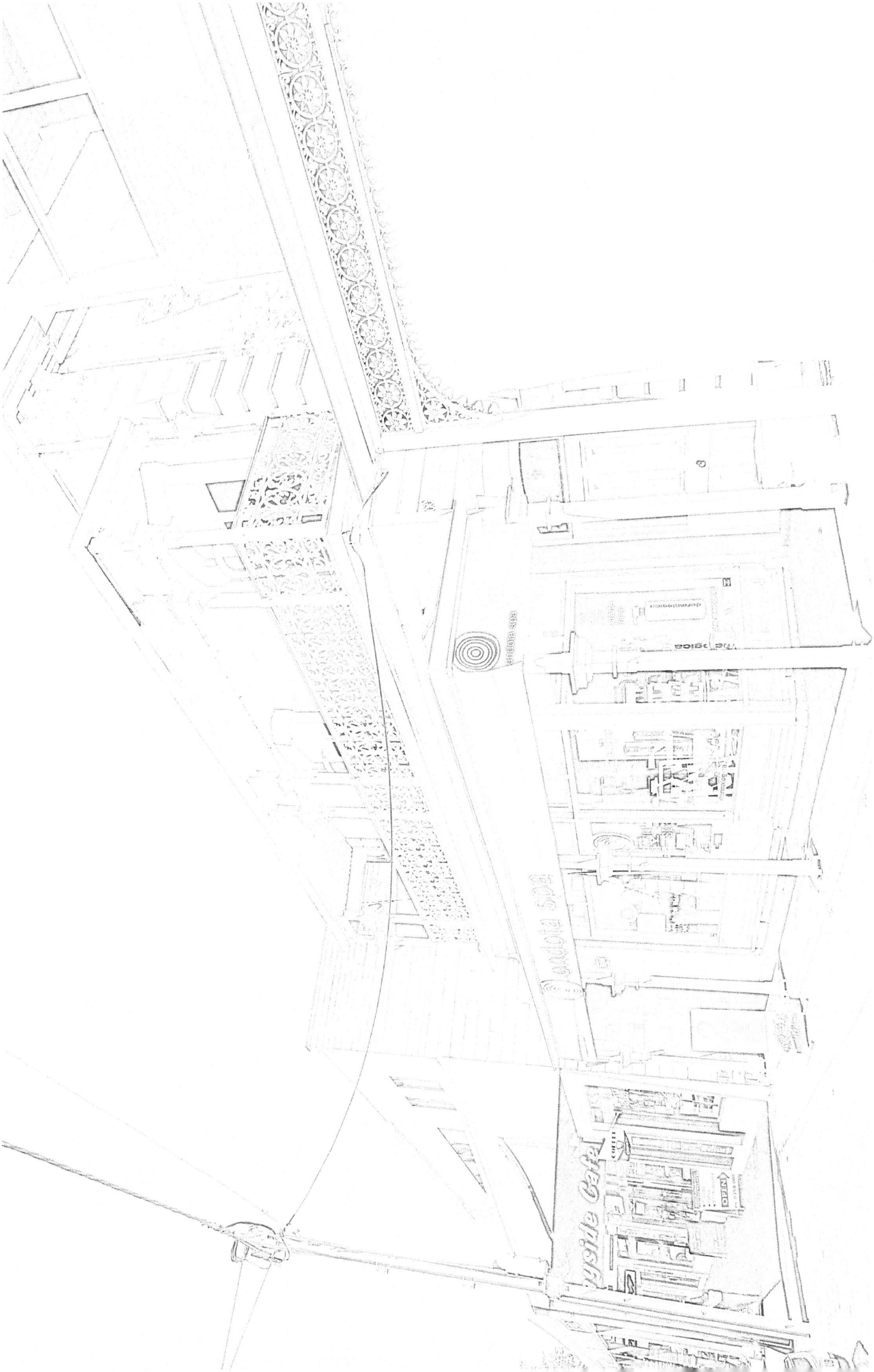
OPEN

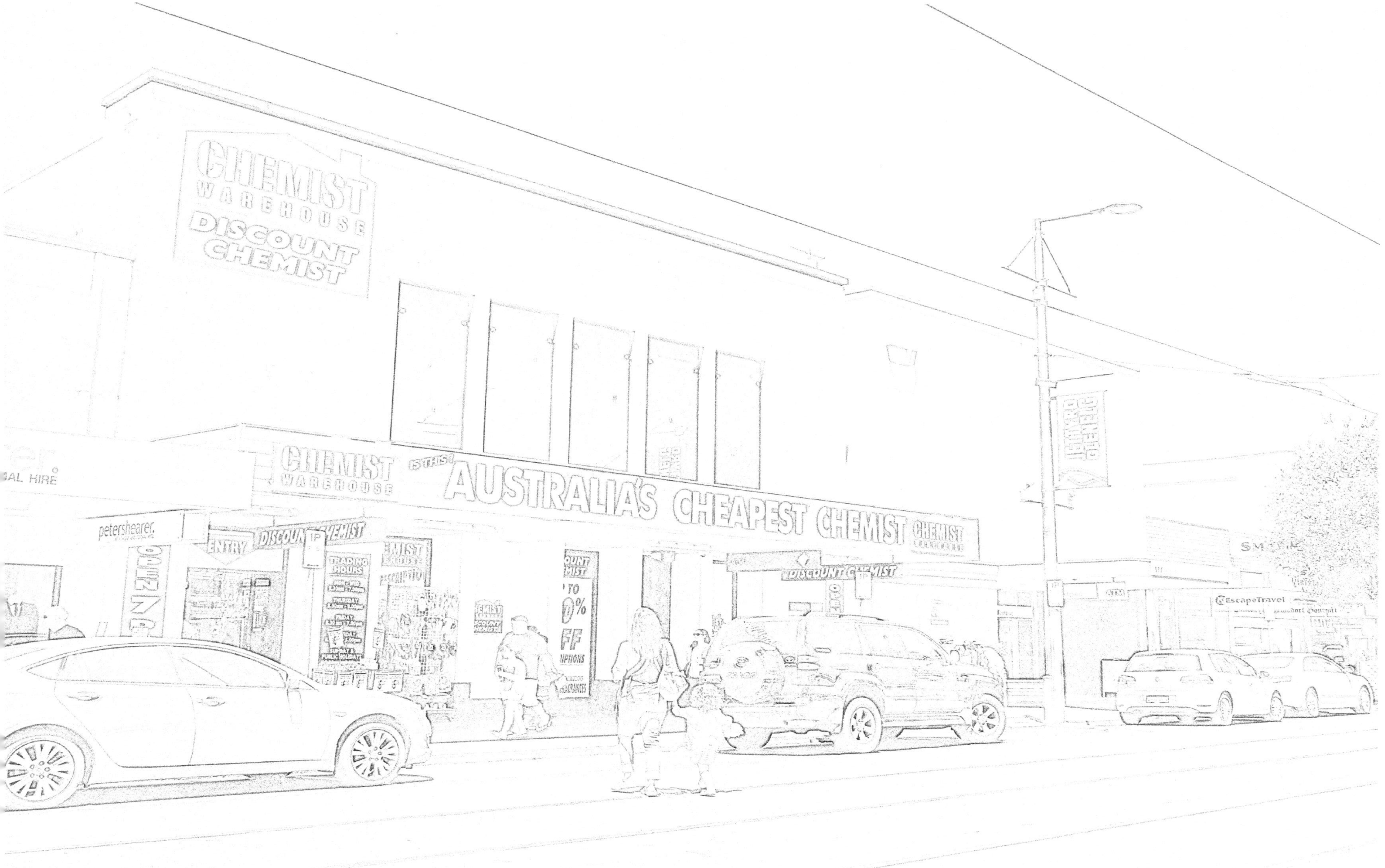
CHEMIST WAREHOUSE
DISCOUNT CHEMIST
CHEMIST WAREHOUSE
AUSTRALIA'S CHEAPEST CHEMIST
DISCOUNT CHEMIST
ENTRY
petershearer.
TRADING HOURS
ATM
EscapeTravel

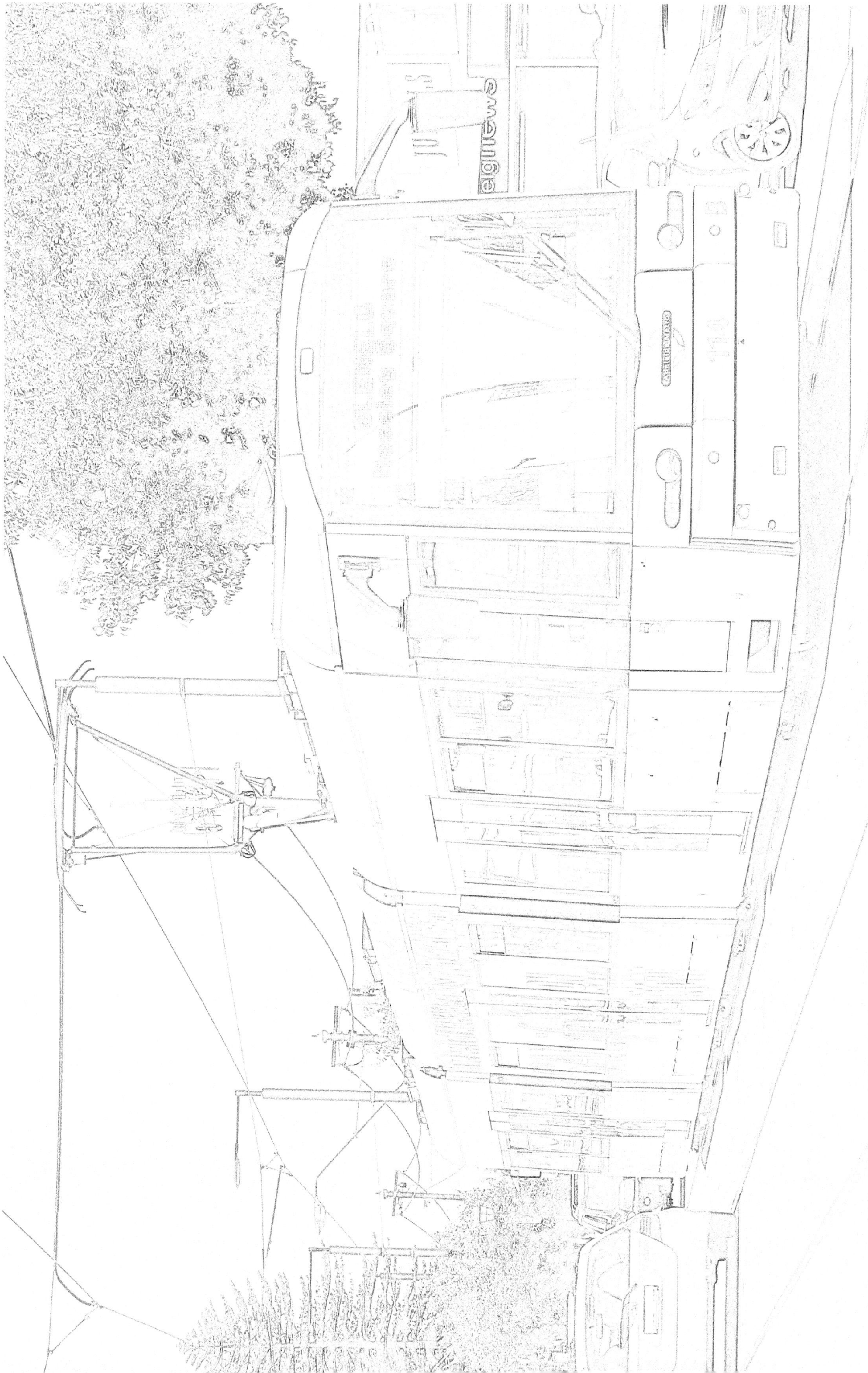

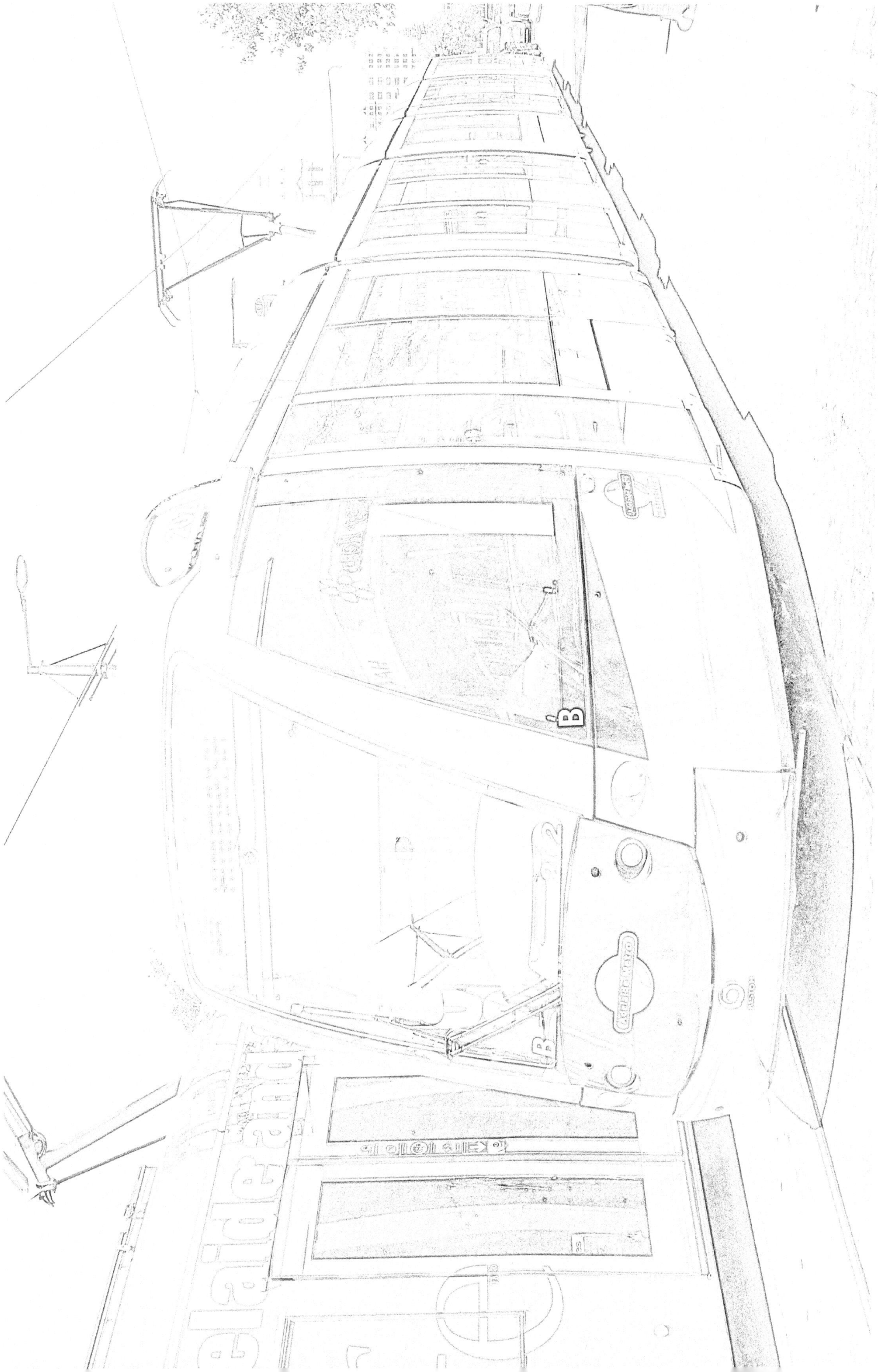

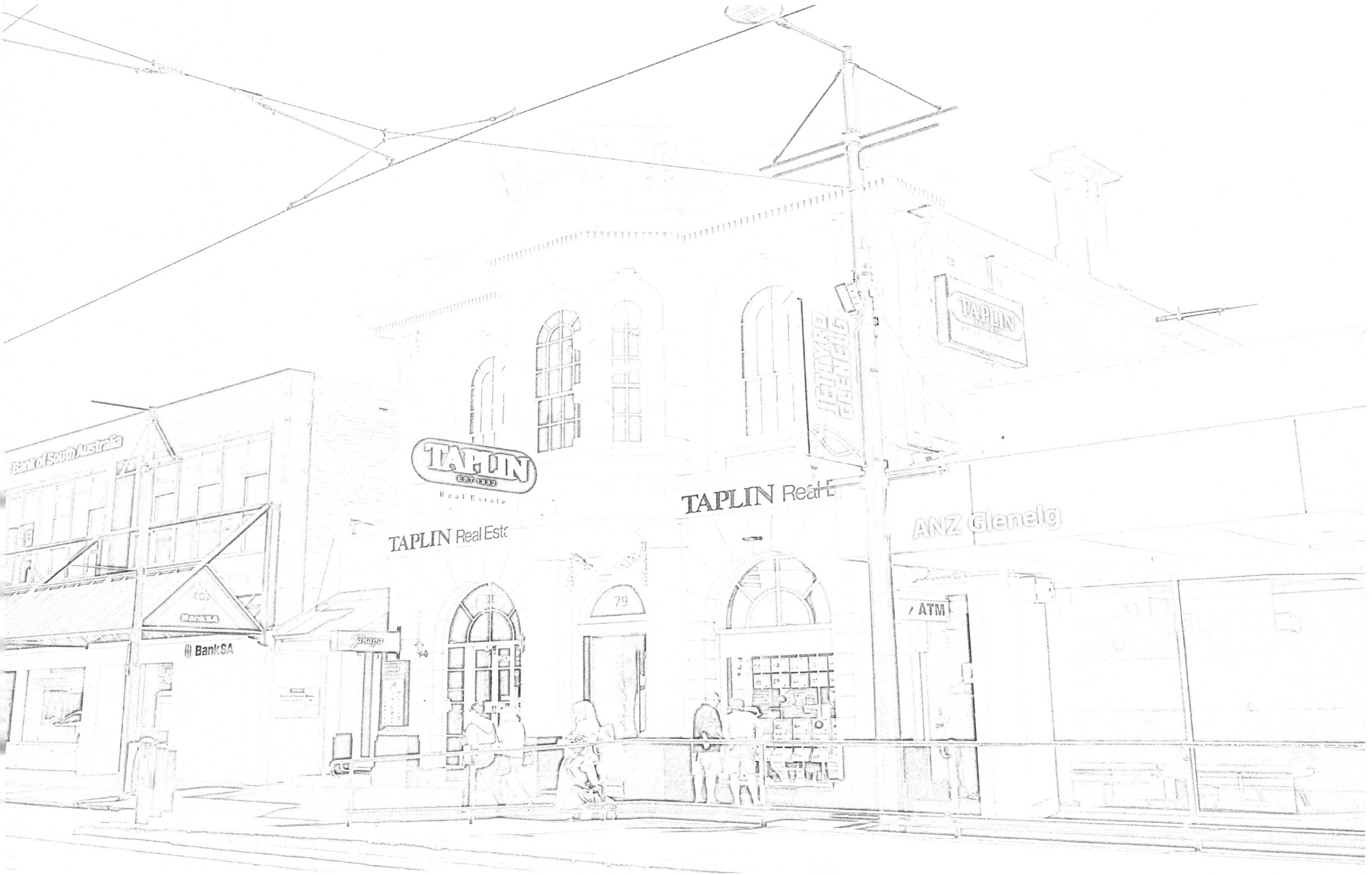
Bank of South Australia
TAPLIN
EST 1932
Real Estate
TAPLIN Real Esta
TAPLIN Real E
JETTY RD GLENELG
ANZ Glenelg
ATM
79
BankSA

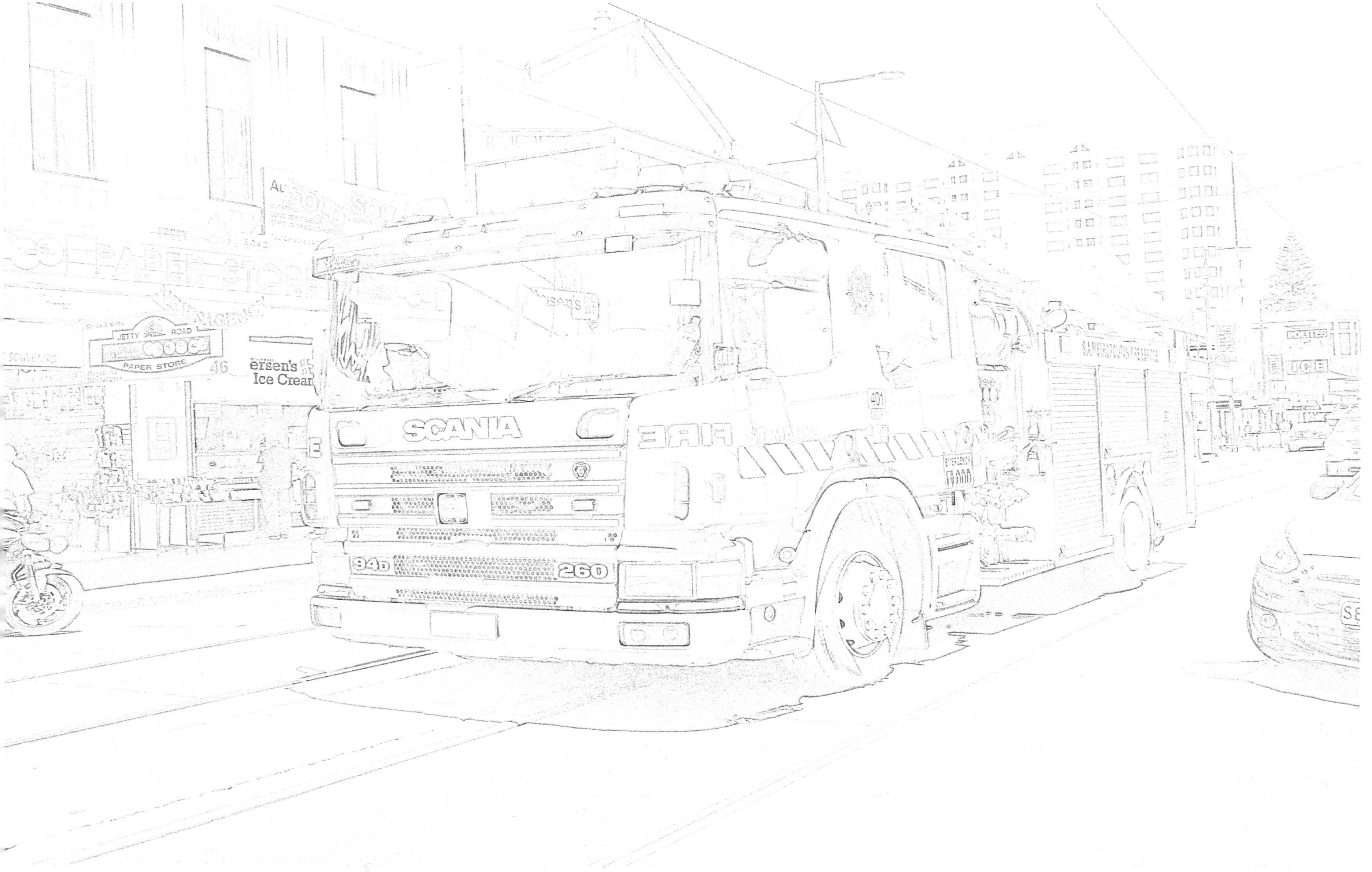
SCANIA
94D
260
FIRE
401
JETTY ROAD
PAPER STORE
46
ersen's
Ice Cream
ICE

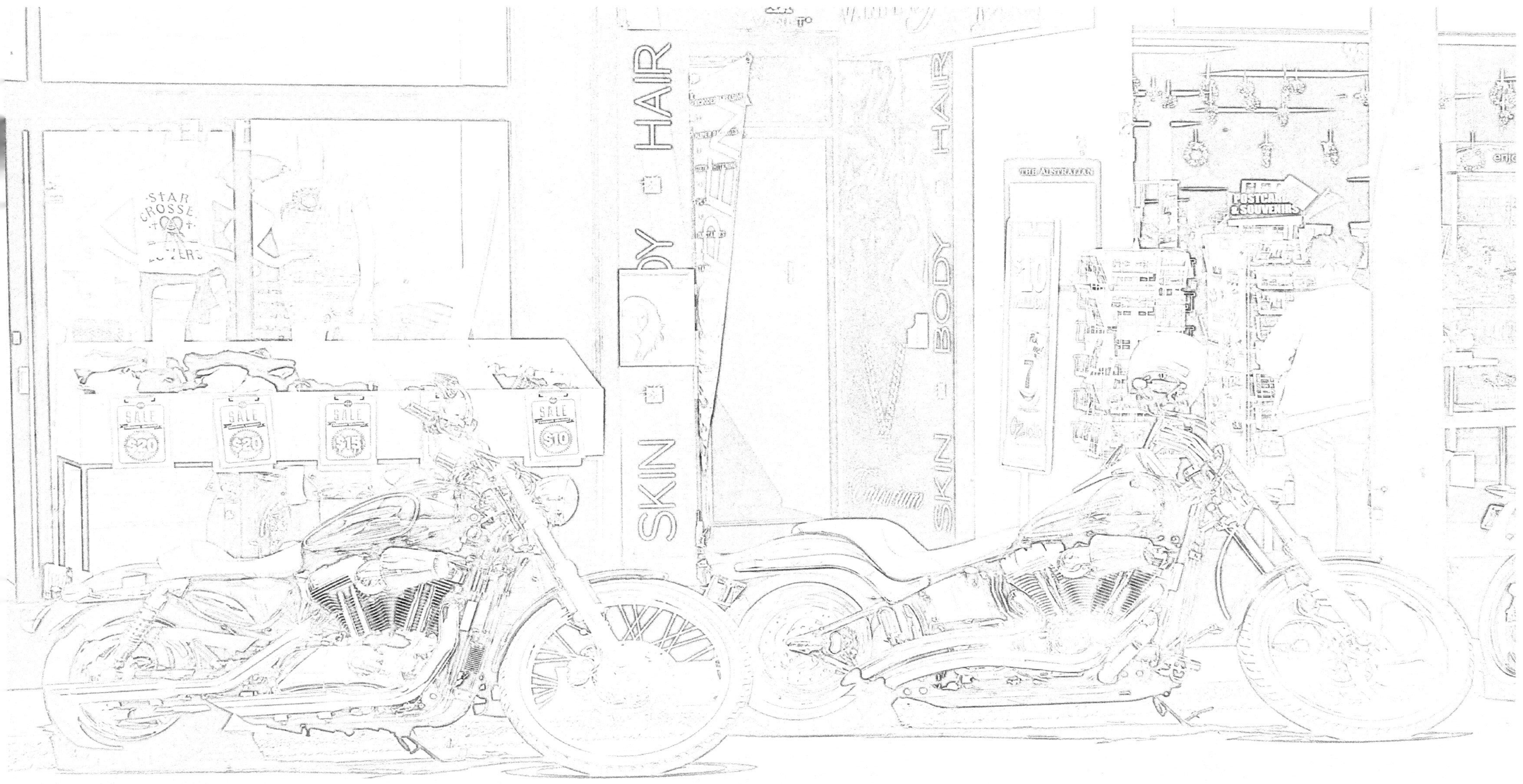
STAR CROSSED LOVERS
SALE $20
SALE $20
SALE $15
SALE $10
SKIN ▪ BODY ▪ HAIR
SKIN ▪ BODY ▪ HAIR
THE AUSTRALIAN
POSTCARDS & SOUVENIRS

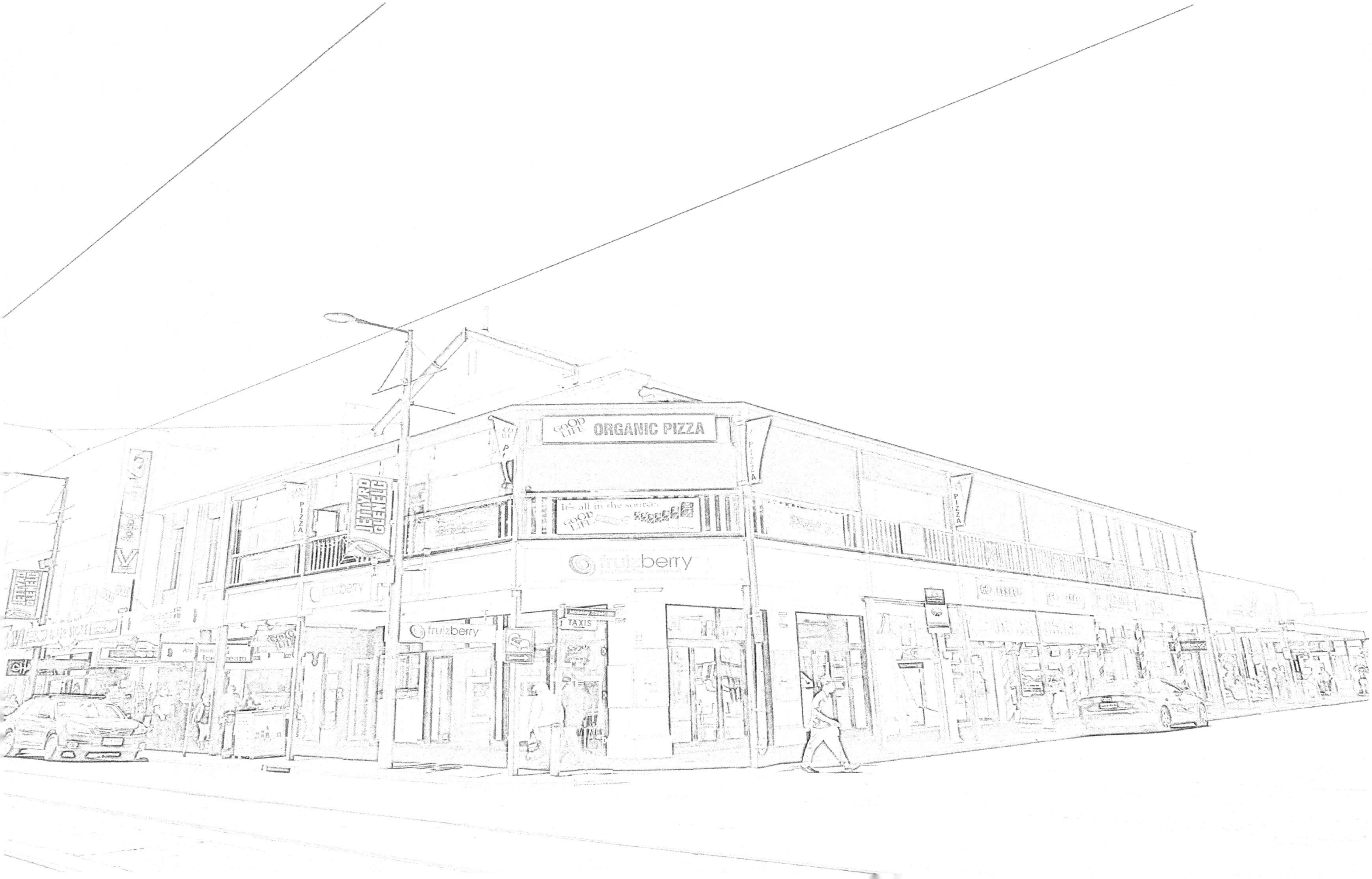
GOOD LIFE ORGANIC PIZZA
PIZZA
It's all in the source.
GOOD LIFE
fruitzberry
TAXIS
fruitzberry
fruitzberry
JETTY RD GLENELG

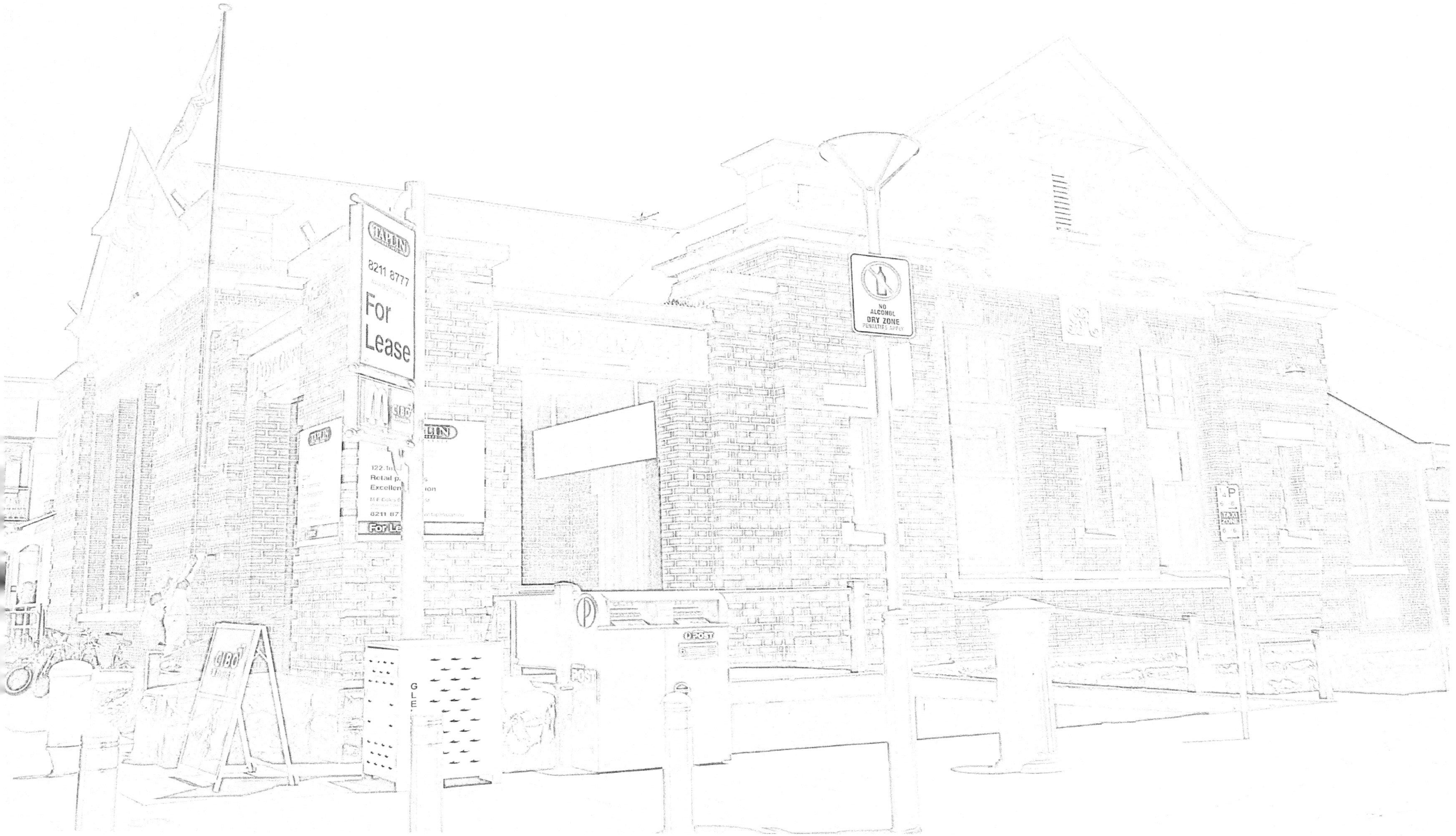

8211 8777
For
Lease
NO
ALCOHOL
DRY ZONE
PENALTIES APPLY
Excellen
For Le
TAXI
ZONE

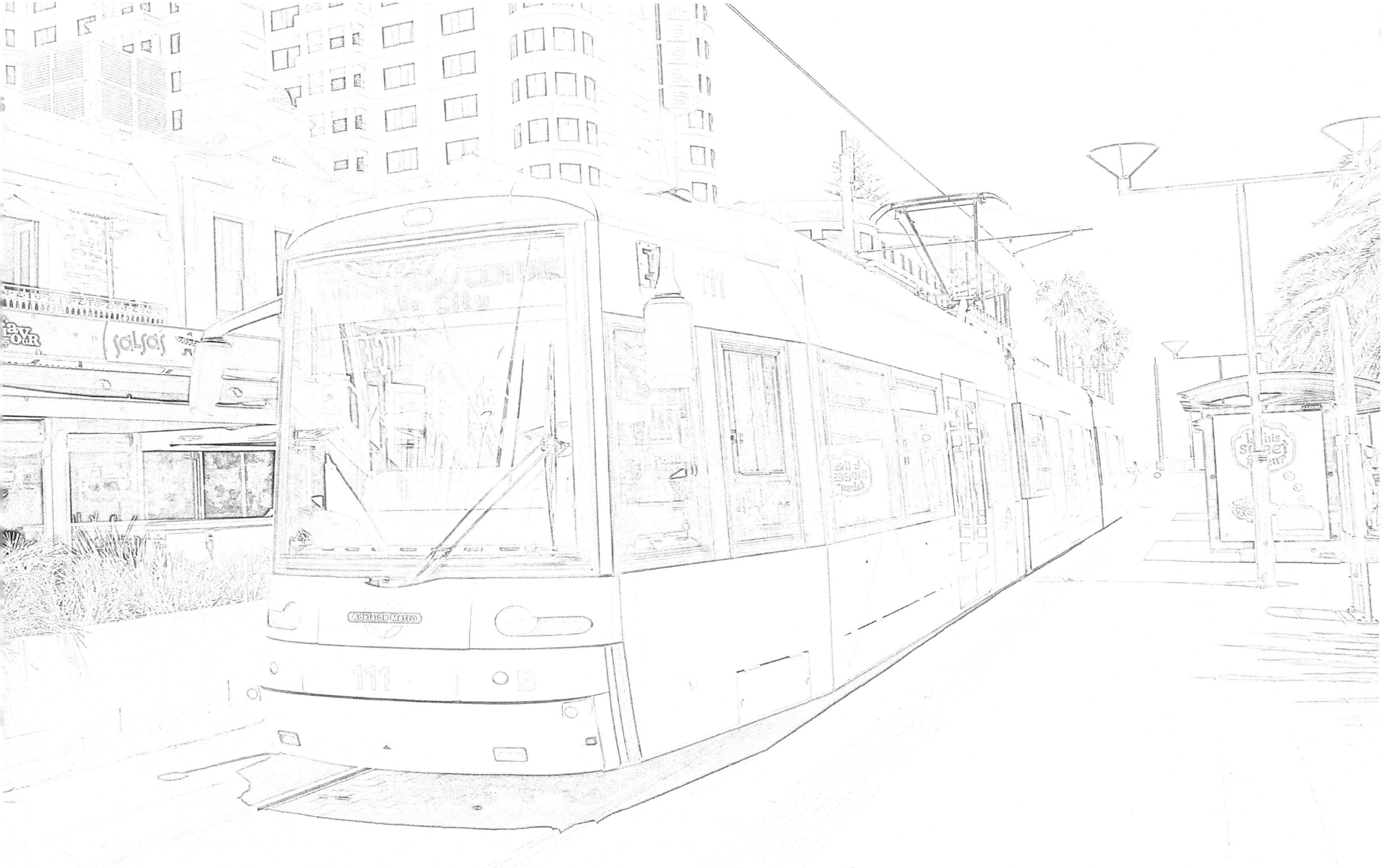
salsa's
Adelaide Metro
111
111 B

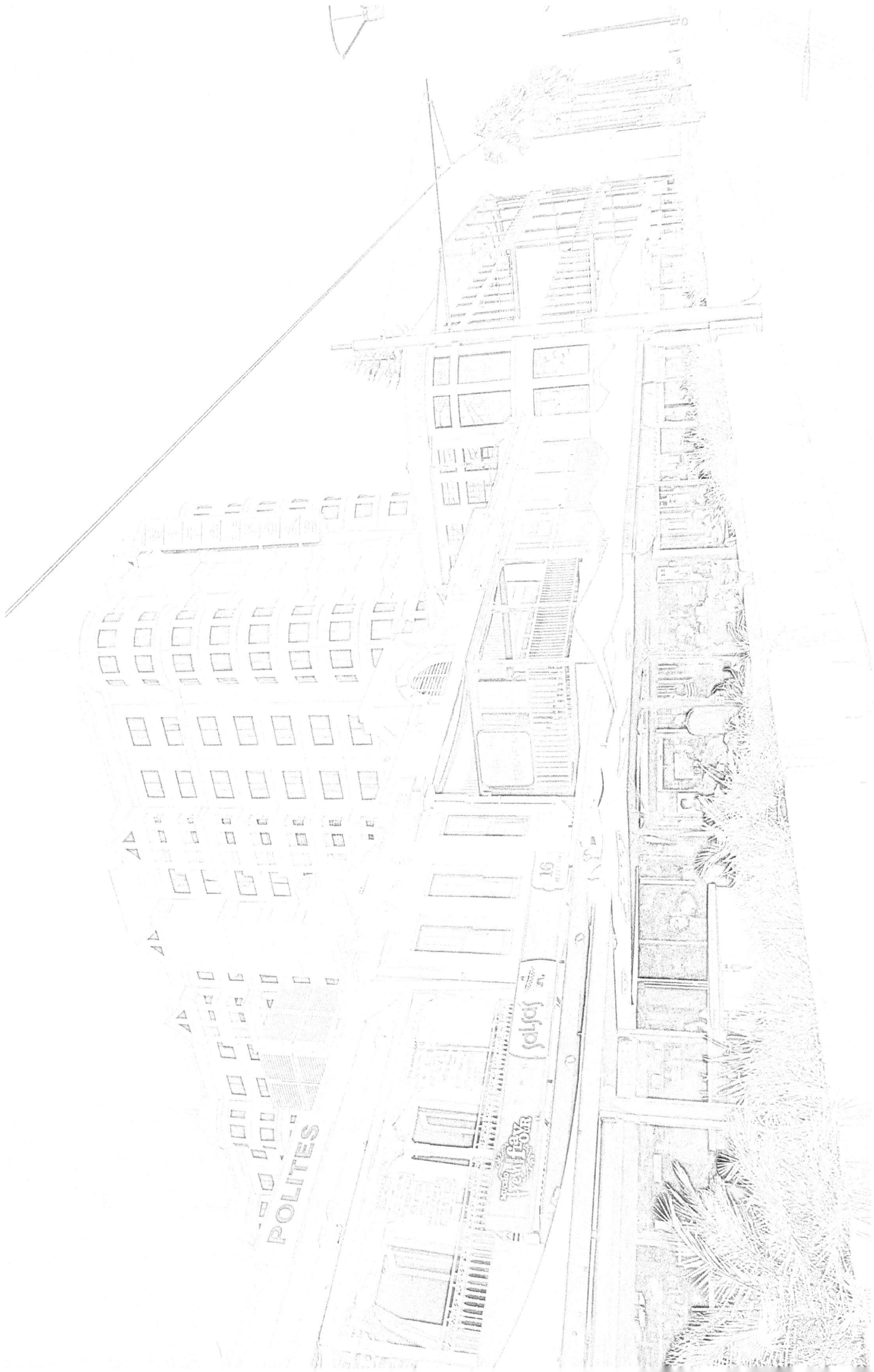
POLITES

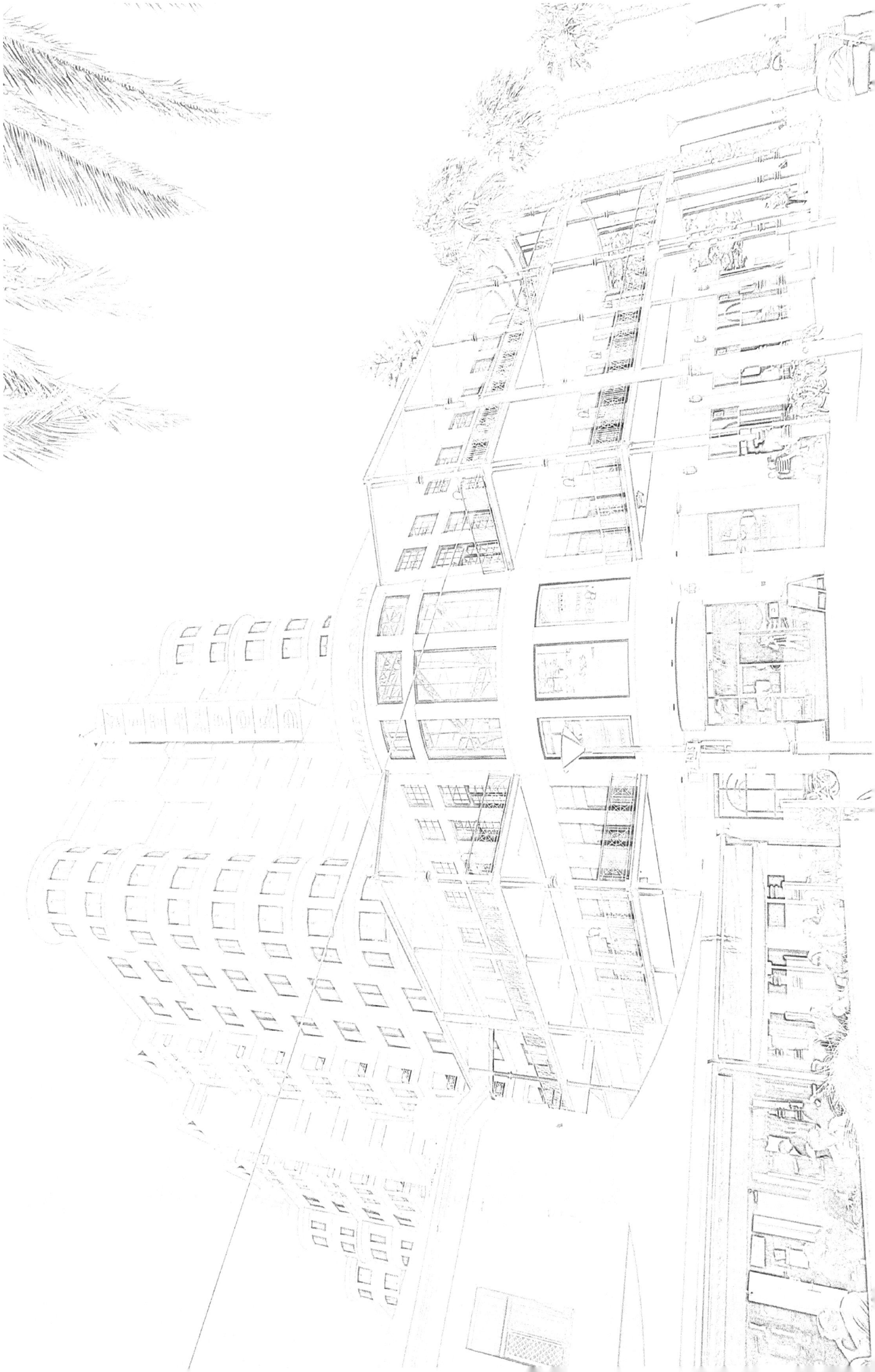

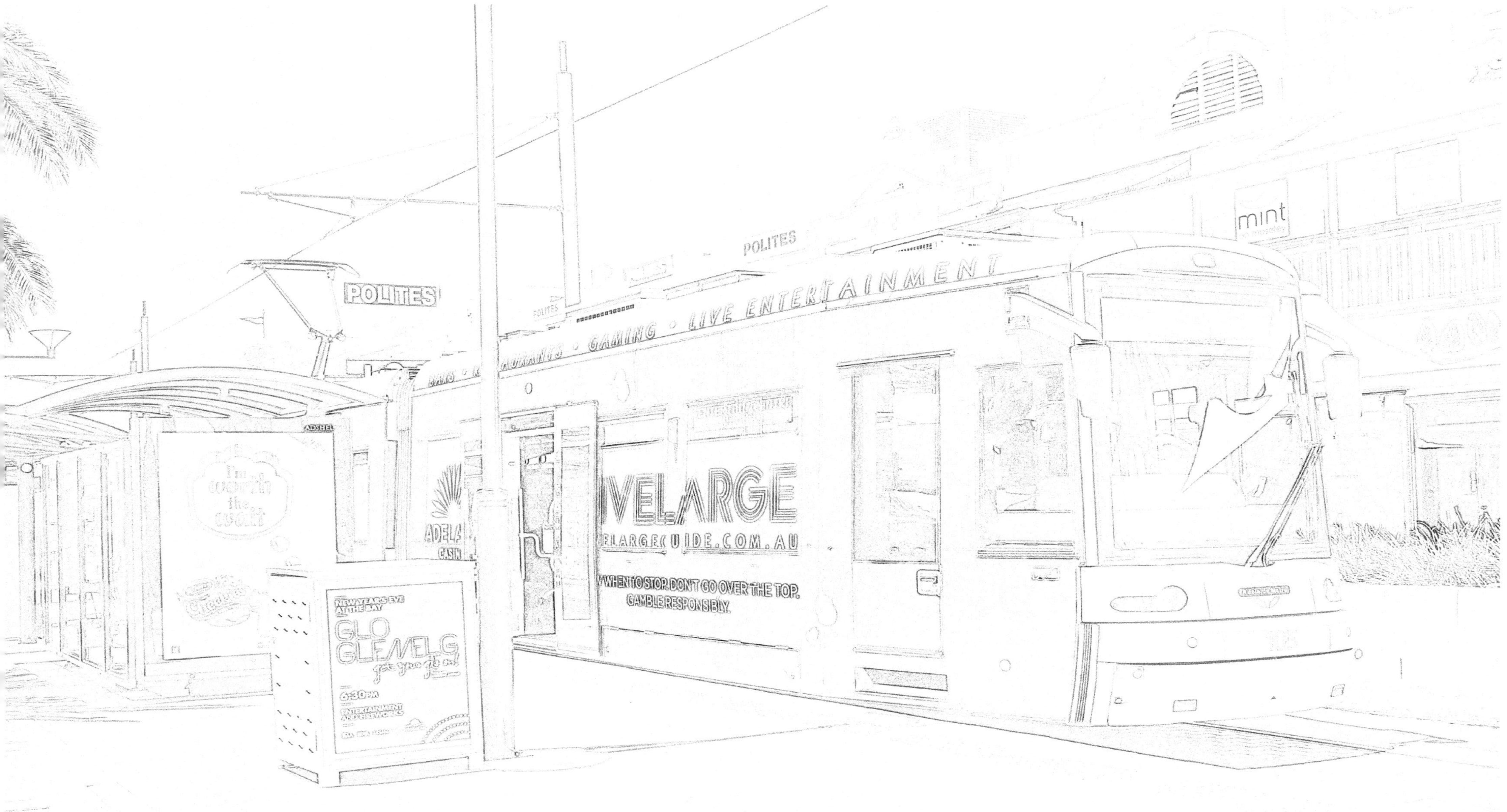
POLITES
POLITES
mint
GAMING • LIVE ENTERTAINMENT
WHEN TO STOP. DON'T GO OVER THE TOP.
GAMBLE RESPONSIBLY.
NEW YEAR'S EVE AT THE BAY
GLO GLENELG
6:30PM
ADSHEL

TOWN HALL.
BAY DISCOVERY CENTRE

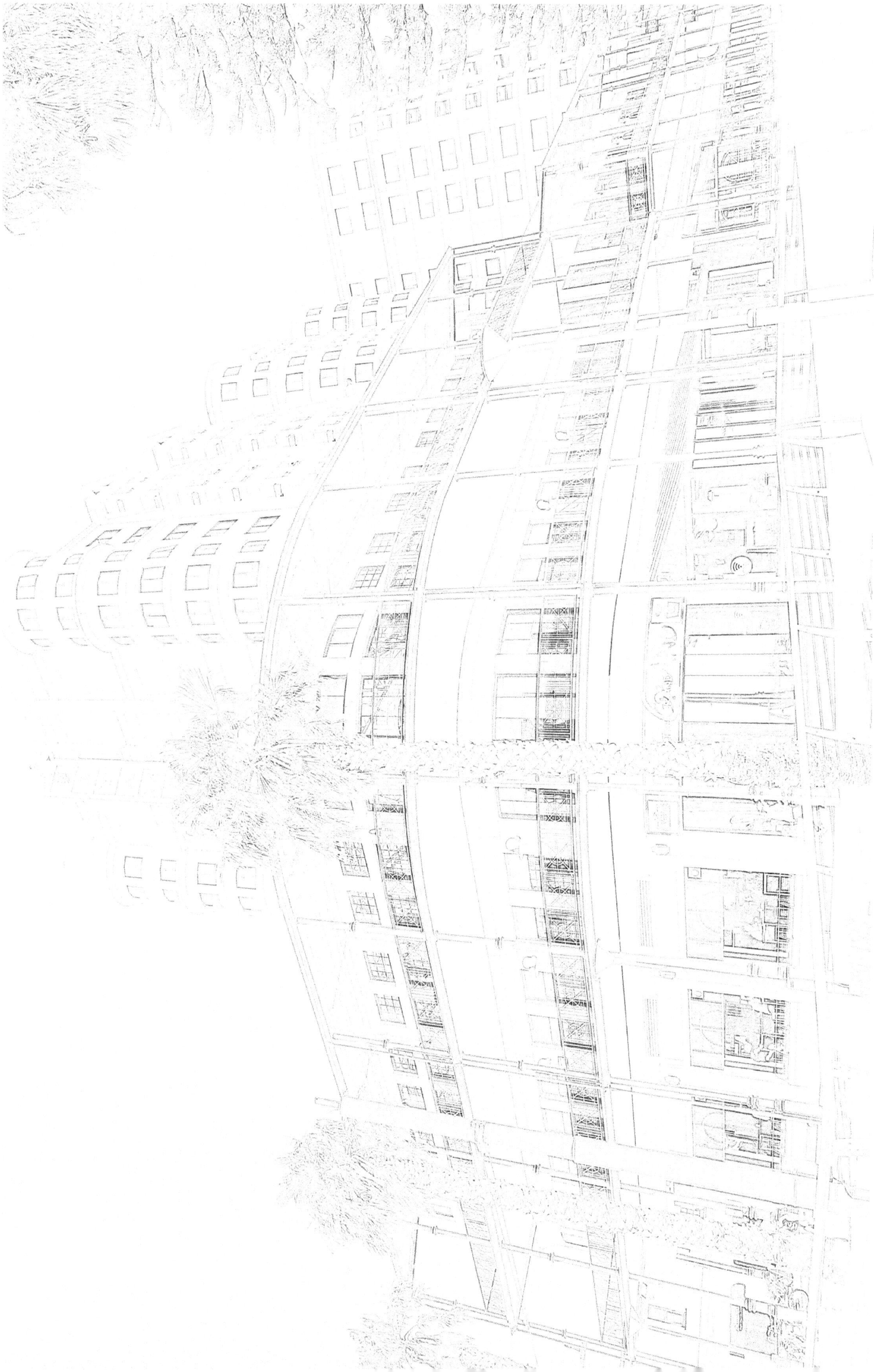

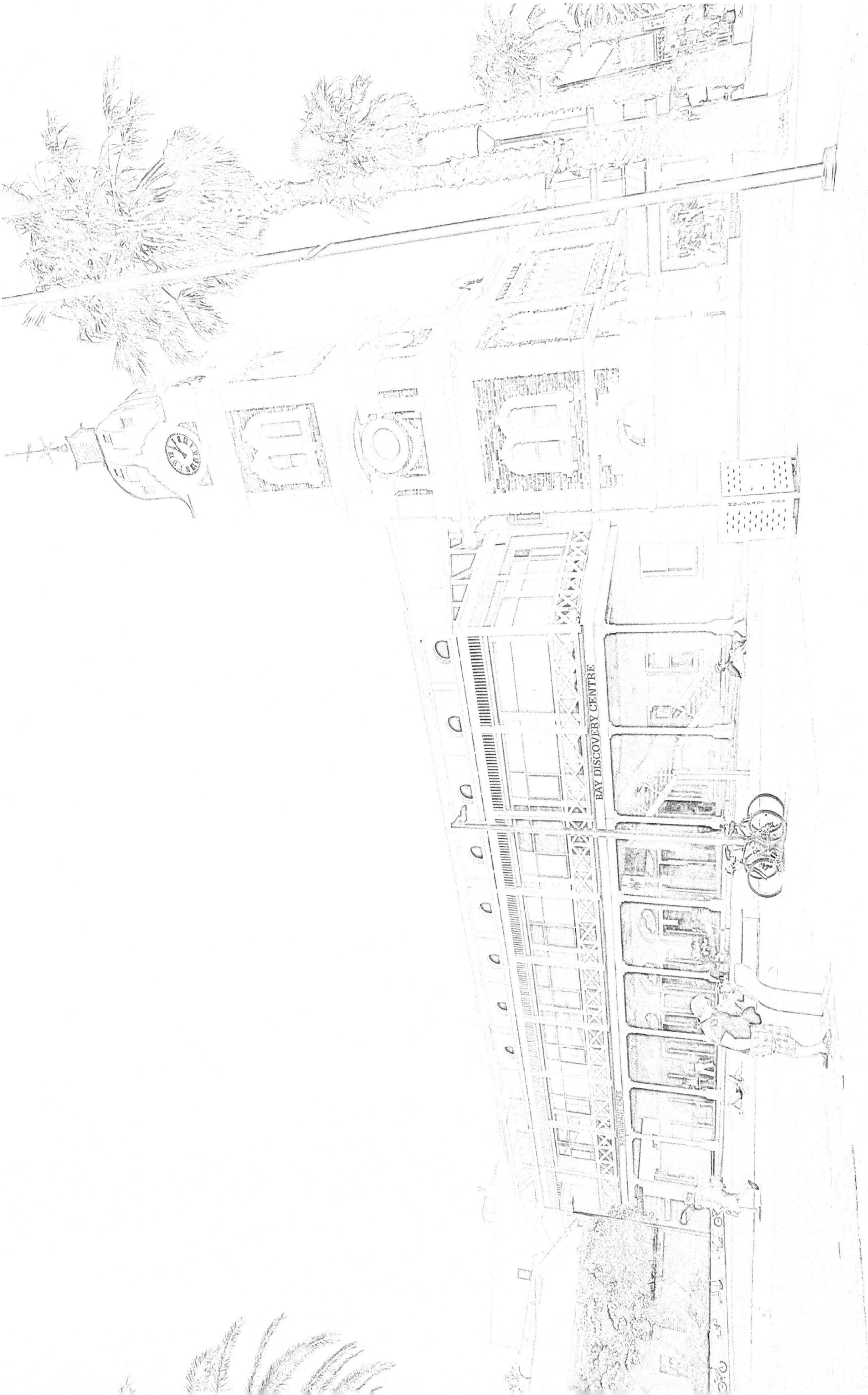
BAY DISCOVERY CENTRE

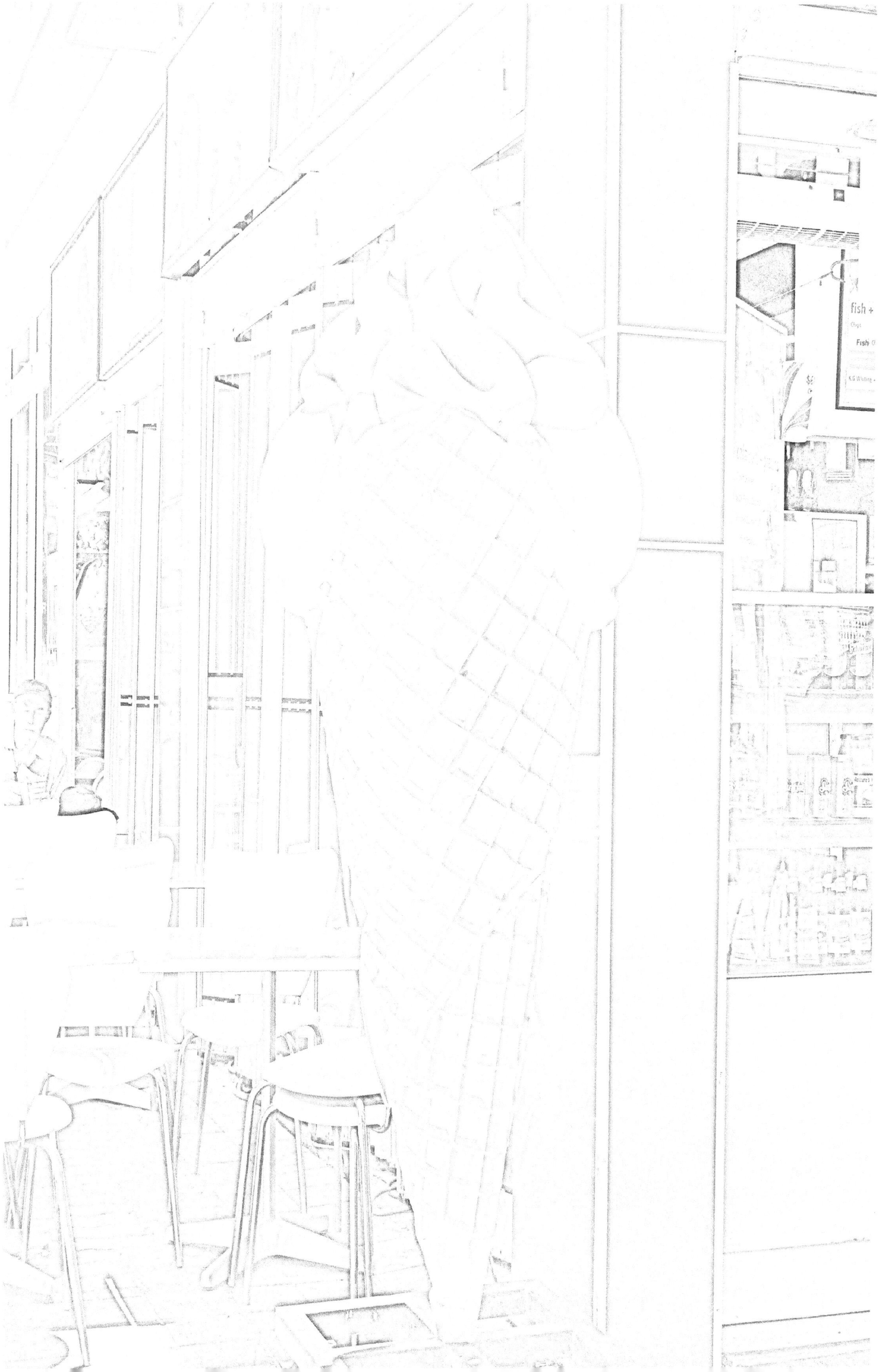
fish +
Fish

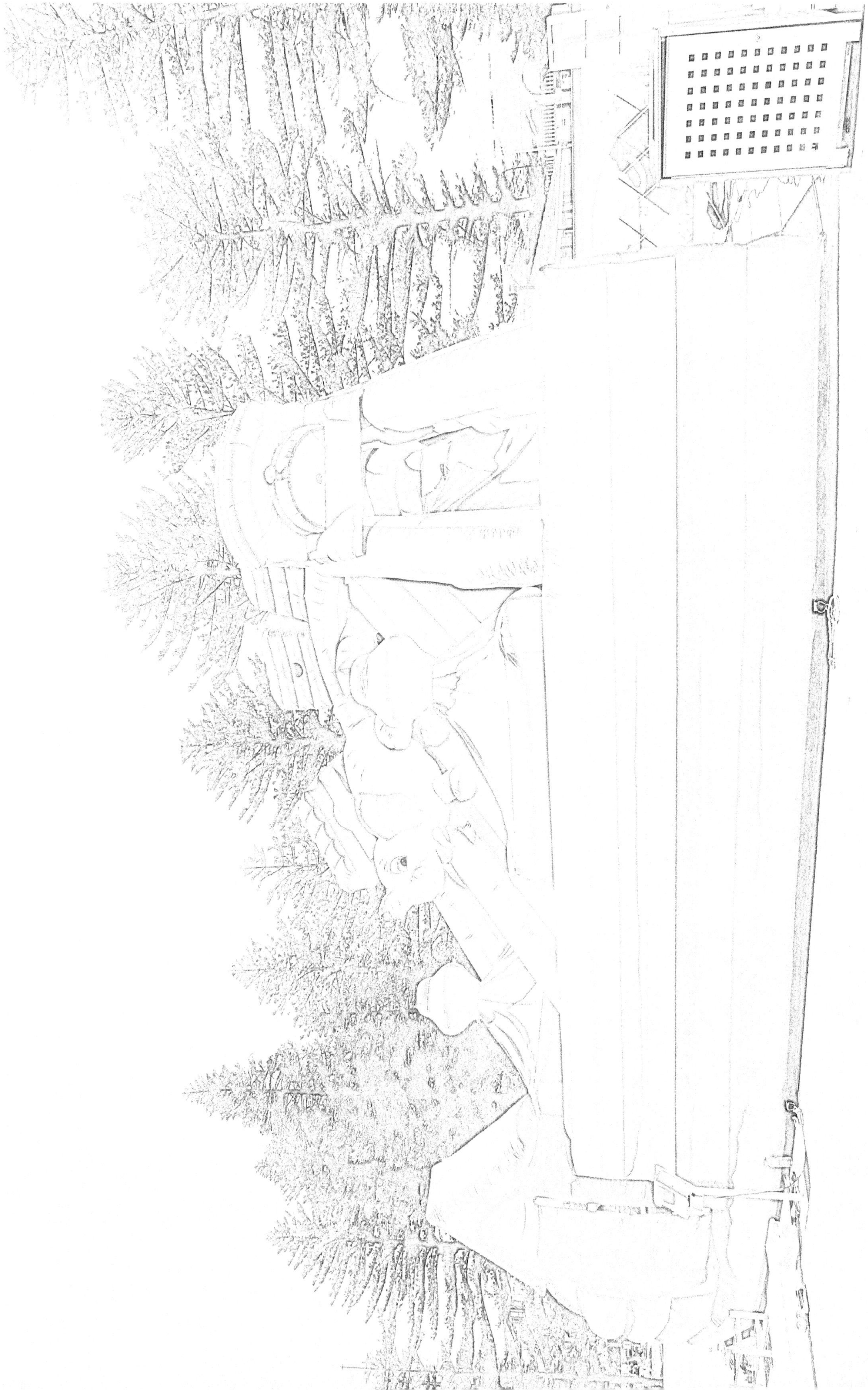

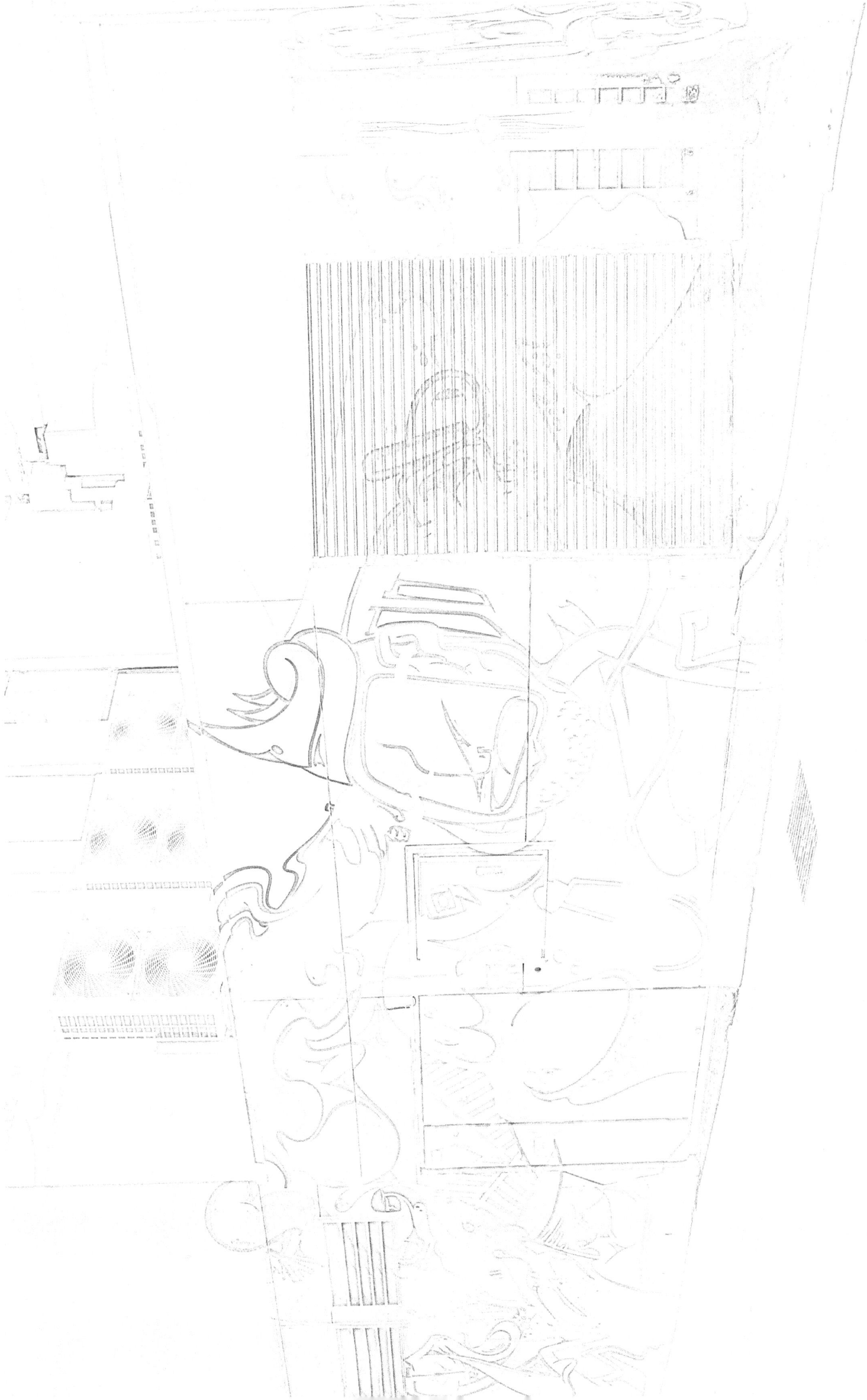

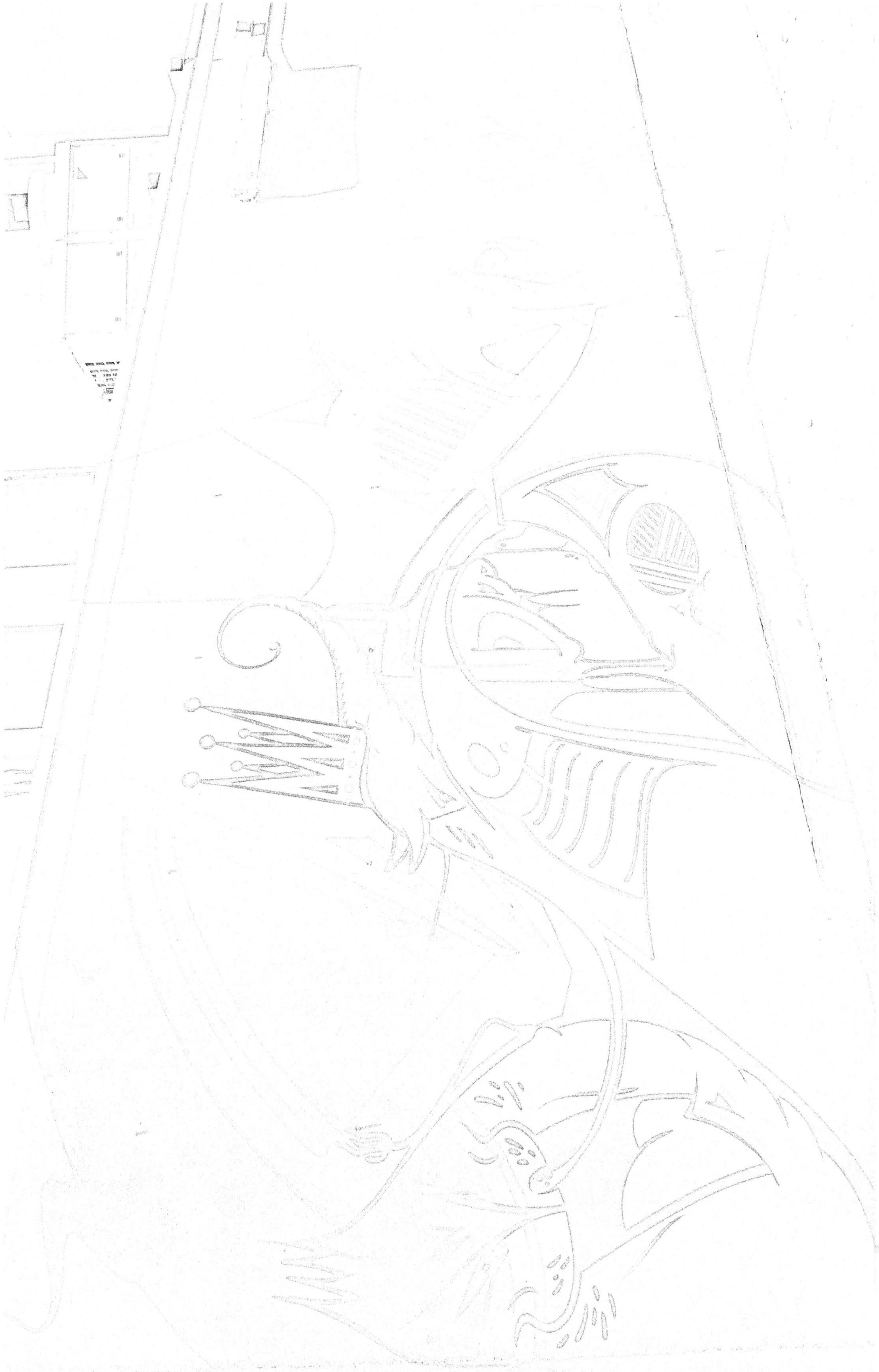

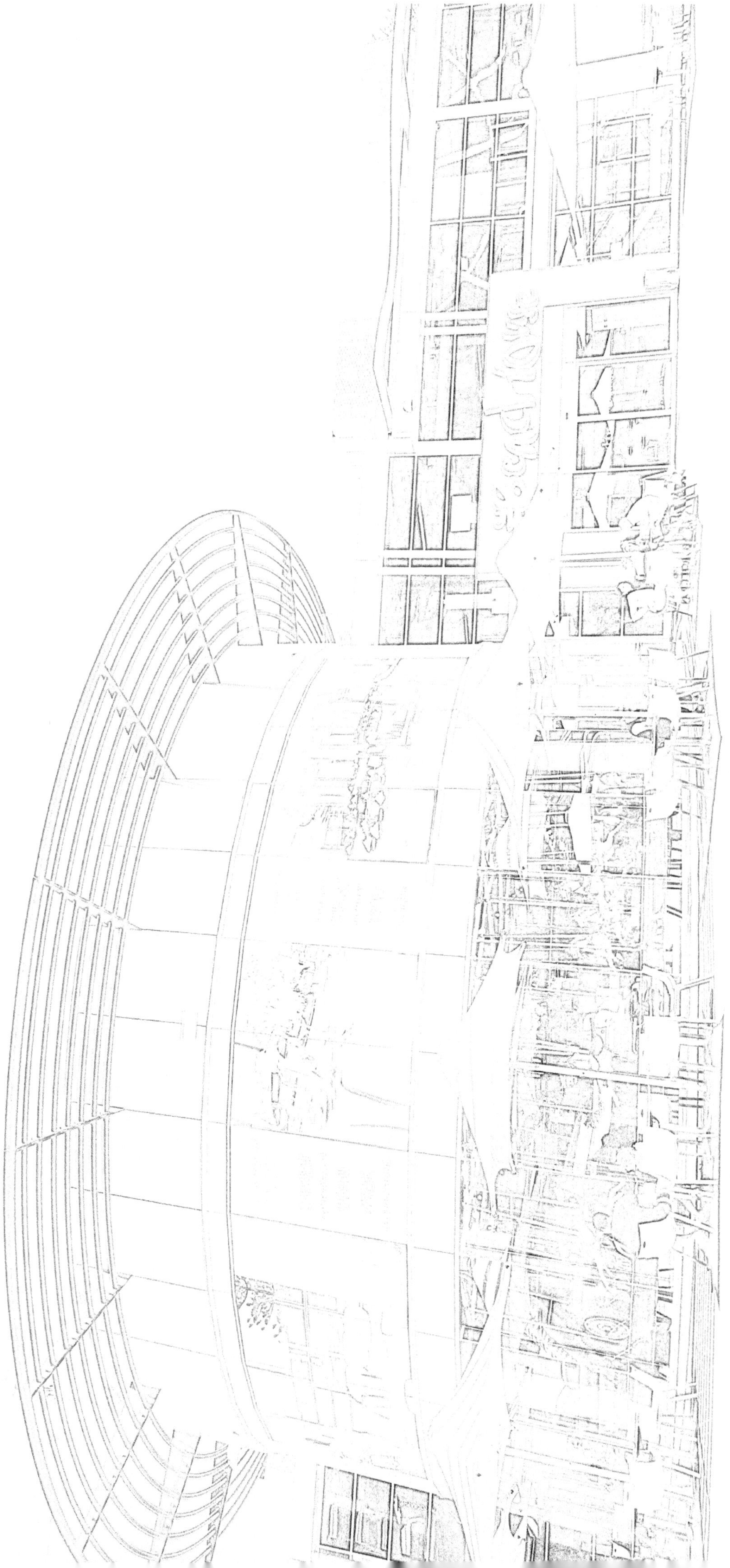

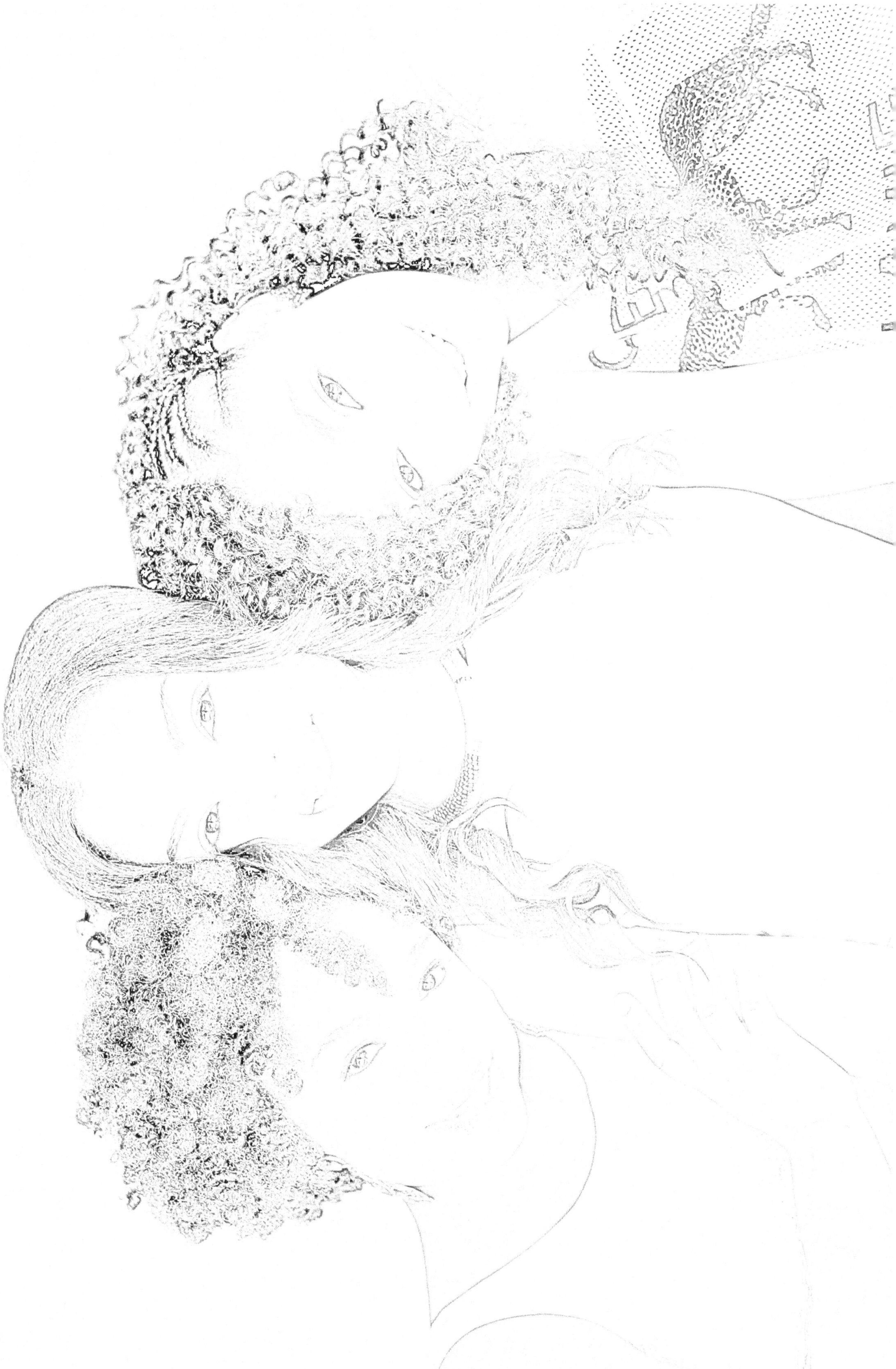

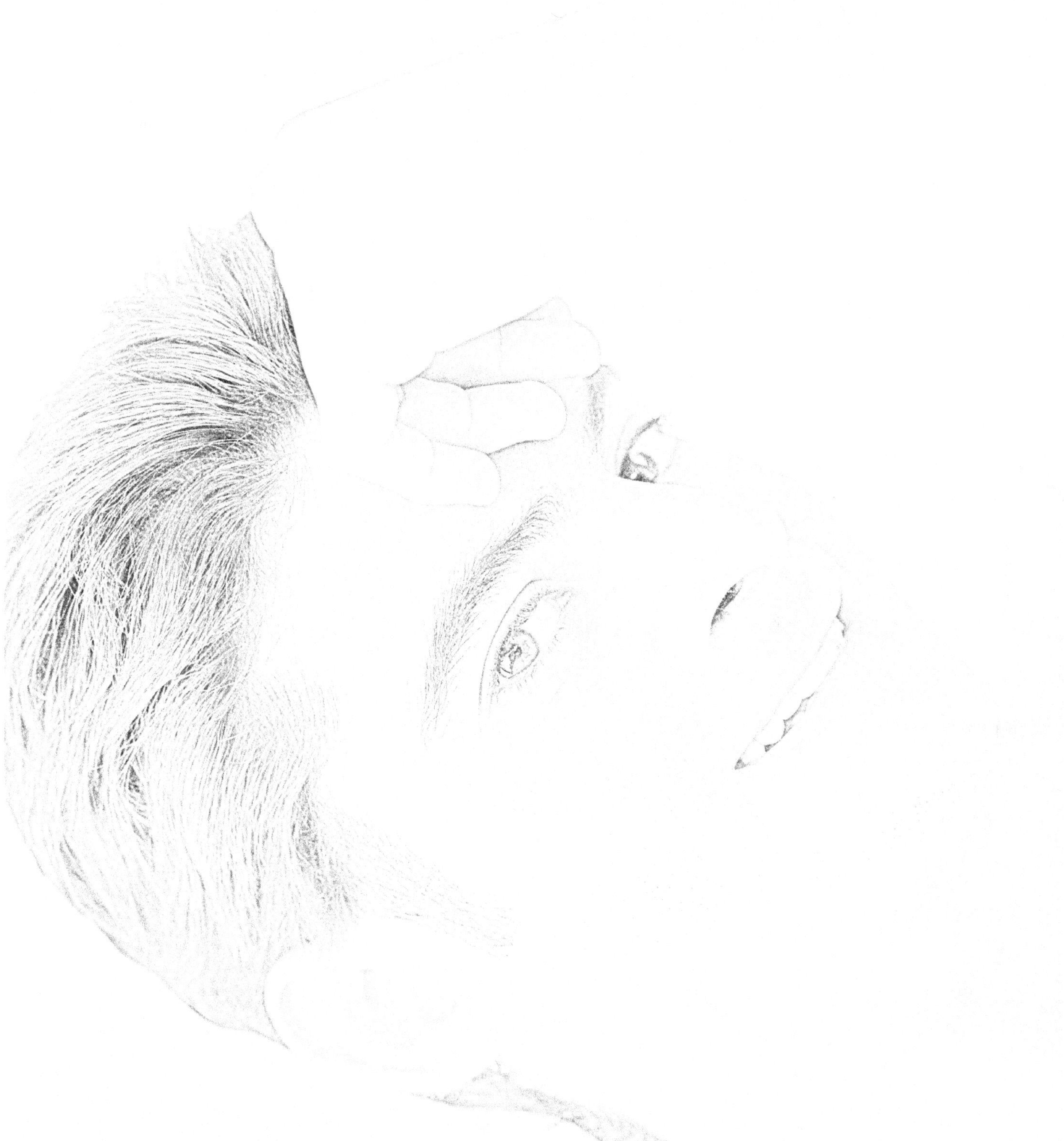

www.ingramcontent.com/pod-product-compliance
Lightning Source LLC
Chambersburg PA
CBHW081059180526
45170CB00005B/1811
* 9 7 8 0 3 5 9 9 3 6 0 1 4 *